Ireland an

Links and Lessons

Do m'iníon, Bríd.

Bhí uirthi céad bhliain a saoil a roinnt le scríobh an leabhair seo, ó thaobh mo chuid ama de. Go mbaine sí taithneamh is tairbhe as, lá éigin amach anseo.

Ireland and Latin America

Links and Lessons

Peadar Kirby

TRÓCAIRE
and
GILL and MACMILLAN

Published in Ireland by

 **TRÓCAIRE**

Catholic Agency for World Development
169 Booterstown Ave.,
Blackrock, Co. Dublin
and
Gill and Macmillan Ltd,
Goldenbridge, Inchicore, Dublin 8
with associated companies in
Auckland, Budapest, Gaborone, Harare, Hong Kong,
Kampala, Kuala Lumpur, Lagos, London, Madras, Manzini,
Melbourne, Mexico City, Nairobi, New York, Singapore,
Sydney, Tokyo, Windhoek

© Trócaire 1992
ISBN 0 7171 1969 6

Design: The Graphiconies
Index: Fergus Mulligan
Print origination by Typeform Ltd
Printed in Ireland by Genprint

Contents

Foreword

The 500th anniversary of Columbus' landing in the Americas has focused attention on the colonial history of that region, a history often marked by plunder and genocide. While acknowledging that the legacy of Columbus' arrival is a complicated one, and that it has helped make Latin America what it is today, both for better and for worse, the voices of the indigenous peoples of Latin America have been raised in protest against any attempt to glorify the anniversary. They, and those who support them in their struggle for human dignity, feel that the occasion should be used to focus world attention on the abysmal situation of crippling poverty, exploitation and injustice in which they find themselves five hundred years after Columbus' historic voyage.

Peadar Kirby's book is an important contribution to a proper commemoration of 1492. He vividly describes the past and continuing exploitation of the majority of the people of Latin America, as well as their efforts to build more just social structures. From an Irish point of view, he draws parallels between the Irish and Latin American experiences of colonisation, thus highlighting the potential for understanding and empathy between our two parts of the world.

The Irish contribution to Latin America has, as Peadar Kirby shows, been substantial – Irish people have played a key role as soldiers, traders and missionaries. Sometimes this role was essentially a colonial one, but many Irish people have helped in the struggles of the Latin American people against oppression.

Trócaire seeks to build on these links by continuing to support Latin Americans in their struggle for dignity and justice. Thanks to the generosity of the Irish people, we were able to allocate almost £1.2 million to development projects in Latin America and the Caribbean in the year to end-February 1991. Through sponsoring books such as this we simultaneously attempt to educate the Irish public about the root causes of the poverty and conflict endured by so many Latin Americans.

As Peadar Kirby outlines, Latin America has deeply influenced sections of Irish society, including the Church and the education sector. We have much to learn from the experiences of that region; this book will make a major contribution to that learning process.

Brian McKeown,
Director, Trócaire,
Dublin, March 1992

Acknowledgments

Far too many people have helped in the preparation of this book to allow mention of individual names. For instance, the book draws on interviews with a large number of people, many but not all of them quoted in the text. To all of these, for giving me of their time and trusting me to give a fair rendering of their views, go my sincere thanks.

The support and help of some deserve special mention. This is true in particular of Trócaire without whose funding this book could not have been written. Thanks must also go to PREAL (Programa de relaciones políticas y de cooperación Europa-América Latina) which funded the initial study of Irish NGO links with Latin America which was the genesis of the present work. It was Sally O'Neill of Trócaire who recommended my name to PREAL and who oversaw the writing of the initial study. To her my thanks go for her encouragement and help with that report as with this book. Andy Storey has been my contact in Trócaire as this book was being written and his active interest in the project, practical help and patience with my many requests, I greatly appreciated. To Trócaire's ever efficient and willing librarian, Ann Kinsella, go special thanks. Her endless willingness to locate obscure newspaper reports of years ago always amazes me. To those in Trócaire who transcribed so clearly my at times obscure taped interviews, especially Mary Nolan, also go my appreciation and thanks.

From a number of those I interviewed I got special encouragement and for this reason I would like to single them out. Dr John de Courcy Ireland's interest in the project as well as help in drawing my attention to particular Irish maritime figures I greatly appreciated. Fr Michael O'Neill of the Columbans showed a similar interest and did me the honour of treating me as if I was writing the definitive history of the Irish missionary movement in Latin America. His careful insights and numerous suggestions were of immense help.

The final and most important mention must be reserved for my wife, Toni. This is not only to ensure continuing domestic peace but for the good reason that without her willingness to shoulder a greater share of the domestic chores than she should this book would never have seen the light of day.

Introduction

The genesis of this book lies in a study of the role of Irish non-governmental organisations (NGOs) in development co-operation with Latin America. The study was done as part of a project to deepen links between the EC and Latin America initiated by Spanish and Portuguese NGOs under the title "Programme on Political Relations and Co-operation Europe-Latin America". Similar studies to the one I wrote on Irish links were written on other EC countries and the results presented at a seminar in Madrid in May 1988. Participants at this seminar expressed surprise at the extent of Irish NGO links with Latin America and at their impact on Irish public opinion during the 1980s, particularly in regard to El Salvador and Nicaragua. These developments in Latin America had not had as major an impact in any other Community country.

The surprise of other Europeans in finding out about the high profile certain Latin American countries had in Ireland at that time could be shared by most Irish people. After all, Ireland has few historical links with the region, little Irish emigration had taken place to that part of the world and, since the foundation of an independent Irish state, little had been done to develop relations. Even the missionary movement, which had fostered Irish links with many African and Asian countries since the late 19th century, has largely neglected Latin America until relatively recently.

Despite the unpropitious background, however, Latin America has probably made a greater impact on Ireland than has any other part of the so called Third World during the 1980s. This is true of the widespread concern of Irish people at events in El Salvador and Nicaragua, a concern strong enough to evoke serious questioning of US policy and actions. But it is also true of the impact on sectors of the Irish Church of new forms of Church organisation and thinking in Latin America, often called the "popular Church". Also, in the field of education, particularly adult education, approaches pioneered by the Brazilian educationalist Paulo Freire and widely applied throughout Latin America, have had an impact in Ireland. Indeed, from observation it appears that sectors of Irish society have been more open to these developments and more interested in them than has been the case in almost any other European country. While this is surprising given the lack of any strong links, it may be accounted for by certain similarities of historical experience between Ireland and all the countries of Latin America. In some ways, our history is closer to that of Latin America than is that of any other European country.

Firstly we share a common experience of sustained and violent colonisation which destroyed the native civilisations it encountered. In this regard, the Irish experience is in particular similar to that of Mexico and Guatemala in northern Latin America and Peru and Bolivia in the southern part, as in these countries the Spanish encountered highly developed civilisations and therefore imposed there the most brutal and sustained repression to ensure their destruction. The long-term effect of that destruction on the psyche of whole peoples continues to exercise a major influence; in recognising it, we Irish can see a certain mirror image of the ways our own past haunts us.

The Latin American states achieved independence therefore as retarded entities with an inherited economic dependence that would impede all attempts at sustained development. Since they reached independence a century earlier than we did, their efforts at national development have a longer history than ours. In the 20th century, our two paths have gone in similar directions. Many Latin American states tried to industrialise through developing local industry to substitute for imports in the 1930s to 1950s; we were following similar policies during the same period. Interestingly, not only were the economic policies similar but the populist, nationalist political movements implementing them in Latin America bore more than a passing resemblance to Fianna Fáil. The 1960s, in Latin America as in Ireland, saw a reversal of these policies and a reliance on multinational companies to deepen industrialisation. Both are also grappling today with the seemingly intractable twin problems of high unemployment and a heavy burden of indebtedness. Even as we enter the 1990s, the similarities continue as Latin America moves towards becoming a free trade area with North America while Ireland deepens its integration into the European Community.

Apart from the similarities of economic policy, at least two other areas of our experience bring us together. One is the presence of the Catholic Church as a major social institution; the developments in that Church in Latin America have already caught the attention of sectors of the Irish Catholic Church. Those working for progressive change in Ireland have much to learn from their Latin American counterparts as to how they could relate to the Church as an institution with potential to be a catalyst for positive change. The second similarity that brings us together is the presence of endemic political violence in both Ireland and Latin America. To the degree that the guerrilla groups of Latin America (with some exceptions, most notably Sendero Luminoso in Peru) have deeper political roots than have those in Ireland and are more willing to move from armed action into political struggle, there is an urgent need that their experience be learnt here.

This book falls into two separate parts, each of which stands on its own though Part One provides the historical context for the involvement of Irish people recounted in Part Two. It is in recognition of the historical similarities between Ireland and Latin America that Part One is written. In dwelling on those areas of historical experience we hold in common, it seems appropriate to entitle it "An Irish Reading of the Latin American Story". The complex questions raised about the appropriateness of the various models of economic development implemented in Latin America and the continuing search for a sustainable model of development fall outside the scope of this book. However, they do serve to remind us that debates and policy development in this country could benefit from interaction with the always lively and far more critical debates raging in Latin America. We have valuable experiences in common and may have far more to learn from one another than we have from so-called developed countries. Similarly, it seems to me that the legacy of colonialism in Latin America, on which the celebrations of the quincentenary of the conquest begun in 1492 have sparked a lively debate (see Chapter 1), has parallels in Ireland to which we should devote attention.

While these similarities motivate the writing of Part One, it stands on its own as an introduction to the history of Latin America. The similarities with Ireland are not adverted to as this would not allow one do justice to the Latin American story in its integrity. Yet the parallels will be obvious to any reader familiar with Irish history. And, before we are ready to learn any lessons from the Latin American experience, I think we in Ireland need to reflect far more systematically on our reality and need to show a far greater commitment to finding a model of development appropriate to our needs. This may be the first lesson to be learnt.

Part Two is devoted to Irish links with Latin America down the centuries. It involves an historical survey (Chapters 7 and 8) which, while not exhaustive, is the first time the major strands of Irish involvement have been brought together and made accessible to the general reader. It is a fascinating story known only in the most general way to most Irish people; indeed, the contribution of the Irish to various Latin American countries is appreciated far more by the Latin Americans than by us Irish. Chapter 9 looks at official Irish links through diplomatic relations, trade and development co-operation. Sadly, despite early promise, the Irish state has neglected Latin America almost entirely. It was therefore left up to the initiatives of the missionary movement and NGOs to develop these links. Their stories are told in Chapters 10 and 11 with special attention to the impact such involvement has had back in Ireland. Chapter 12 ponders the possibilities for building on these links in the future.

Finally, a note on terminology. In a general work of this nature, it is tiresome to draw the reader into terminological debates that may be of little relevance or import. The use of one set of terms, however, deserves comment. These are terms that relate to states of development or underdevelopment. I do not believe that there is a "developed" and a "developing" world. These terms in fact mask a reality of exploitation through which some one quarter to one fifth of the world's people grow richer at the expense of the rest, many of whom are being steadily pushed to the brink of survival. Yet, the terms in common use offer little choice in a narrative of this type if one is not to confuse the average reader. It is with great reluctance, therefore, that terms like "Third World" or "underdeveloped" are used and they are not to be taken as implying that the countries of the South (in this case Latin America) can reach "development" through following the prescriptions of the countries of the North. As Part One should indicate, the reality is far more complex and poses fundamental questions about the meaning of development and how to achieve it. These are questions on which Irish and Latin Americans have much to offer one another.

Peadar Kirby,
Dublin,
February 1992

Part One

An Irish Reading of the Latin American Story

"We may not be a better people than others, but we are at least more human, being formed from the most varied types of humanity. We are a people which over the centuries has suffered the most brutal and constant poverty and oppression, still heavily soiled by fantasies of Europe, still bearing in abundance the scars of slavery and colonialism, still very badly served by alienated and faithless intellectuals; but we are a people already opening up to the future, already on the march to create its own civilization, driven by an insatiable hunger for fullness, happiness and joy."

— Darcy Ribeiro, Brazilian anthropologist and novelist[1]

Chapter 1

A Region in Search of Itself

"The real struggle for Latin America is, as always, a struggle with ourselves, within ourselves. We must solve it by ourselves."

– Carlos Fuentes, Mexican novelist[2]

The date 1492 is rightly seen as marking one of the key turning points of European history, as important as the French Revolution in 1789 or the Russian Revolution in 1917. But, as the Spanish government found out when it began to plan for the 500th anniversary of the event, there is less agreement on what this date actually marks. In a speech to the General Assembly of the United Nations in November 1982, the then Irish Ambassador, Noel Dorr asked: "Is it not something of an exaggeration to speak so confidently of it [the first landing by Christopher Columbus in the Americas in October 1492] as 'the discovery of America'?" He reminded his listeners that "the New World was already inhabited at that stage and that other voyagers from Europe had probably reached there by then, even if they made little of their discovery."[3]

In his 1982 speech, Noel Dorr anticipated in diplomatic parlance the increasingly forceful criticisms expressed by many Latin Americans about plans to commemorate the 500th anniversary of the "discovery of America" (see Appendix I). For many Latin Americans are becoming increasingly aware that such a phrase betrays a continuing sense of European superiority towards them, a continuing colonial attitude. "Our existence might have been a discovery for you but we were already here for some 35,000 to 40,000 years," many native Americans reply. The outcry from Latin America at plans to mark the continent's "discovery" forced the Spaniards, the official sponsors of the event, to find a rather more euphemistic title and so it became known as the "500th Anniversary of the Encounter of Cultures". It was the leading Latin American historian, Enrique Dussel, who underlined the euphemism of such a title when he pointed out that what happened in effect was that "one culture encountered another and the first destroyed the second."[4]

The lively debate sparked off throughout Latin America by plans to mark the 5th centenary of Columbus' first landing in the region was entirely appropriate. It shows the degree to which, over recent decades, Latin Americans have begun to appropriate their own ambiguous historical legacy, to face its appalling violence and destructiveness and to chart their own indigenous paths towards development. In the words of Enrique Dussel, it shows the extent to which significant sectors of Latin American society have begun to examine their reality, not standing alongside the *conquistadores* on the decks of their caravels but rather standing on the beaches with the indigenous peoples (misnamed Indians by the Europeans) as they watch the slow approach of these "floating houses" as they called them.[5] Looking at Latin American history from the standpoint of its victims gives rise to an entirely different reading of it than does looking at it from the standpoint of the conquerers.

Rather than acquiescing therefore in any triumphalistic celebrations, many Latin Americans have forced a consideration of the true nature of the event which gave birth to present-day Latin America. The murdered Salvadorean Jesuit, Ignacio Ellacuría, entitled a book he wrote on the subject (and published posthumously) *Descubrimiento ó Encubrimiento* drawing attention to the common roots of the terms "discovery" and "cover-up". For many Latin Americans, what to Europeans was a "discovery" was instead a massive "cover-up", the cover-up of what Eduardo Galeano called "five centuries of the pillage of a continent", the subtitle of his classic work *Open Veins of Latin America*. What truly happened when Europe met the peoples of this vast continent has been condemned by many historians as the greatest genocide in the history of humankind when, according to some estimates, a population of some 100 million was reduced to no more than 10-12 million in the first 70 years of the conquest. This was caused by war and plunder, by the diseases introduced by the Spaniards and, over a longer period, by the virtual slavery to which the native peoples were reduced.

Legacy of conquest

Setting the historical record straight is no mere academic exercise, however. For many see the legacy of this genocide in the warped and violent societies which today make up the continent, societies characterised by gross inequalities in wealth distribution, by widespread poverty and disease, by massive underemployment and by a deep-rooted racism which re-inforces rigid class divisions. Indeed, even in specific ways, the very same genocide practised by the *conquistadores* continues today in the elimination of native peoples such as the Yanomami people of the Brazilian Amazon. A people who have lived in the same area for over 3,000 years, they are now facing extinction from the inroads of goldminers who, if they do not kill them physically, poison their water-courses, rape the women and children and transmit to them diseases such as influenza, malaria and tuberculosis, all deadly to the Yanomamis.

What is at stake therefore in re-appropriating as fully as possible what Latin America has suffered is the attempt by Latin Americans to re-possess their own continent for themselves. This is made so much more complex by the fact that what is today Latin America is, in the words of Brazilian anthropologist and novelist Darcy Ribeiro, a European invention. Its name comes, not from anything indigenous, but from the Florentine mapmaker Amerigo Vespucci. The languages through which it communicates, Spanish and Portuguese, are those of its conquerers. Only in Paraguay is a native language, Guaraní, a recognised and widely-used language of urban society though the Mayan languages of Guatemala, Quechua in Peru and Aymara in Bolivia are widely used rural languages. Its religion too is European, though at times the beliefs and practices of native religions are clearly visible behind the facade of Catholic devotions. Only where there is a large black population, as in Brazil, Cuba and Haiti, is there encountered in the cults of candomblé, macumba and voodoo the widespread practice of something approaching a native religion, with their syncretistic mixtures of African and Christian elements. The religions of the native peoples have grown progressively weaker as many of them, the lowland peoples of the jungle regions, are pushed to the very edge of extinction.

But while the culture that we today call Latin American contains many native elements intermixed with its European forms, the class structure has been less flexible in allowing native peoples progress up the social ladder. Here generalisations are impossible as the racial mix varies from country to country, depending on the racial origins of most of its population. But what can be stated is that even in countries with a large indigenous population as is the case in Mexico and Guatemala in the north and Peru and Bolivia in the south, the ruling class both politically and economically is predominantly European in racial origin. It is remarkable the extent to which the descendents of the early waves of Spanish and Portuguese have managed not only to keep their racial purity but also their social and economic power though they make up only a tiny percentage of the population. The lower down the social ladder one goes in Latin America, the more native (or black in those countries where large numbers of black slaves were brought in) becomes the predominant racial strain in the population. It is at this level, rather than among the ruling elite, that racial intermixing has taken place.

Racial intermixing

The deepest sense in which Latin America is a European invention, however, is the very make-up of its population. For the Latin American as we know her or him today is the result of the greatest racial intermixing that history has yet produced, an intermixing produced by the European conquest. Most Latin Americans are of mixed blood but the mixtures are so varied that they can be said to have produced a new racial type. The basic mixture, of course, is of European and native which from the beginning of the conquest was very common due to the small number of Spaniards and the even smaller number of Spanish women in America. So extensive was this that even in countries with a large population of native origin, many have some element of European blood in them. Only among the smaller tribal groups, as for example the Amazonian peoples, does one encounter relatively pure racial groups as they have been little integrated into the surrounding society.

The second racial strain which has become a major component in the make-up of the contemporary Latin American is the black strain, the result of years of importing African slaves, particularly to work the sugar plantations of Brazil and the Caribbean. It is now reckoned that over the four centuries from the conquest until slavery was finally abolished in the 1880s, between 12 and 15 million black slaves were imported into the Americas. Apart from Brazil and the Caribbean states, the black presence is today a recognisable feature of the populations of Peru, Venezuela, Colombia, the Guyanas and some Central American countries.

An Asian strain is recognisable in the Japanese of Brazil, the Chinese of Peru and the East Indians of the Caribbean, some of them brought in by the British in the last century as clerks, overseers and indentured labour. Finally, the European strain has been broadened over the 19th and 20th centuries by the influx of

18

English, Italians, Germans, French and even Irish to various Latin American countries. These have given rise to distinctive racial and cultural groupings as, for example, the Irish-Argentines, the Anglo-Uruguayans, the Germano-Chileans or the Franco-Brazilians.

While this racial intermixing has some similarities to what happened in North America, there the races tended to preserve their own racial distinctiveness and whites have tended to intermix more exclusively with other European races. In Latin America, on the other hand, one can speak more truly about the creation of a new people, "no longer indigenous, nor African, nor European", in the words of Darcy Ribeiro. For him, the result has been neo-Americans "whose vision of the world, life-styles and aspirations... make them one of the most variegated branches of the human species. The fusion of people from all corners of the earth has created here peoples of mixed race preserving in their ethnic and cultural features heritages drawn from all the sources of the human race."[6] This particular result of the European conquest, he writes, is a matter for rejoicing. "What deserves attention is not only the blood shed, but also the creature conceived and born in it."[7] Many outsiders also find the Latin Americans an enormously attractive people, warm in humanity, rich in resourcefulness, sharp in vision and strong in their capacity to struggle.

Self-discovery

Yet, while rejoicing in their rich humanity, Latin Americans are also painfully coming to terms with the cultural legacy of the conquest, of this European invention we call Latin America. Eduardo Galeano goes so far as to say that "Latin America is gravely ill with alienation; it sees itself through the eyes of those who exploit and oppress it. Latin America has been trained in resignation and fear; it has been taught to betray itself."[8] Instead of affirming its own distinctiveness, it has all too often been content to copy from what it regarded as its European (or latterly its North American) betters. Nowhere is this better expressed than in the Ecuadorean exhibit sent to the Paris Universal Exhibition in 1867. While the country has its own rich tradition of indigenous art and crafts, its government sent copies of the most famous works of European artists. This example could be multiplied many times over, not only in cultural matters but also in politics, economics and in Church life. As a European invention, Latin America was not expected to offer the world anything distinctive except for its precious metals and its luscious fruits and vegetables..

If Latin America has therefore begun to offer anything distinctive to the world over recent decades, it has done so to the extent that it has begun to discover itself, appropriate its own distinct experience and unleash its own creativity. One need point only to the Cuban and Nicaraguan revolutions and the mystique surrounding their leaders, to liberation theology and the Church of the poor or to such writers as Pablo Neruda, Gabriel García Márquez, Octavio Paz, César Vallejo, Isabel Allende, Carlos Fuentes or Mario Vargas Llosa as evidence that such a process is indeed taking place.

In their introductory essay to a collection on the theme of 1492-1992, the theologians Virgil Elizondo and Leonardo Boff speak of Latin American cultures being "condemned to be cultures of resistance rather than creative and liberating."[9] It is true that what characterises Latin America as a whole is its cultures of resistance, cultures that can be traced back to the early days of the conquest and whose presence is clearly visible in the struggles of the intervening half millennium. Yet, as the examples mentioned above also indicate, out of the cultures of resistance elements of real creativity and liberation have grown. In tracing the region's history, we are seeking to highlight the cultures of resistance but also to identify these elements of creativity and liberation.

Footnotes

1. Darcy Ribeiro, 'The Latin American People' in *1492-1992: The Voice of the Victims*, London, SCM Press, 1990, pp 18, 19
2. Carlos Fuentes, from his Harvard Commencement Speech, June 1983
3. Noel Dorr in a speech to the General Assembly of the United Nations, 29 November 1982. The text of most of the speech is reproduced in Appendix I.
4. Enrique Dussel, 'Los sentidos de conmemorar 1492' in *500 Años del Cristianismo en America Latina*, Santiago, 1990, p 12 (translated by PK)
5. Ibid., p 12
6. Darcy Ribeiro, op. cit., p 27
7. Ibid., p 19
8. Eduardo Galeano, in an interview in *Latinamerica Press*, 19 February 1987, p 3
9. Virgil Elizondo, Leonardo Boff, 'Editorial: The voices of the Victims: Who will Listen to Them?' in *1492-1992: The Voice of the Victims*, op. cit. p ix

Chapter 2

Pre-Columbian America and its European Conquest

"Take back your Bible and give it back to our oppressors. They need its moral precepts more than we because, since the arrival of Christopher Columbus, America has had imposed on it, by force, a culture, a language, a religion and values which belong to Europe."

–Aymara indigenous in a letter to Pope John Paul II, 1985[1]

When Christopher Columbus first set foot on what he called the island of San Salvador (probably what is now Watling Island in the Bahamas) on 12 October 1492, he had no idea of the vast land mass that lay before him. Thinking he had landed somewhere off the coast of China in the Indies, he proceeded to call the first native peoples he encountered, who were of the Arawak race, Indians. They were, he reported back to King Ferdinand of Spain, peaceful people, loyal and without greed and ripe for conversion to the true faith.

Unfortunately, this benign attitude did not last long. On his first voyage, Columbus and his men discovered some alluvial gold and gold ornaments. The 1,200 settlers he brought with him on his second voyage at the end of 1493 soon tired of trying to cultivate the land of Hispaniola (today's Dominican Republic and Haiti where Columbus founded his first settlements) and instead turned to hunting the natives and looking for gold. By the time of his third voyage in 1498, Columbus found the escapades of the Spaniards had provoked the peaceful natives to the point of war. Instead of being able to calm the Spaniards, however, Columbus was forced to appease them in their hunger for gold and granted them land and native slaves. The form the conquest was to take was already being established.

The continent that Columbus stumbled upon and which was unknown to Europeans had already been inhabited for some 35,000 to 40,000 years. The first inhabitants had come in the Ice Age across the Bering Straits from Asia to America whose two land masses were then joined. They quickly spread throughout the continent and evidence of early settlement has been found from Alaska to southern Chile and Argentina. By the time the Europeans arrived, it is estimated that some 1,500 to 2,000 different languages were spoken among the native peoples of the Americas, from the nomadic peoples of southern Argentina to jungle tribes of the Amazon basin, from the warlike Caribs of Venezuela and the Caribbean to the pacifist Chanes of Paraguay.

Early settled cultures

While many of these remained at a relatively primitive stage of development, it was in the plains of northern and central Mexico and the oases of Peru's coastal desert where the continent's first settled agricultural life developed around 5,000 BC. In Peru, these developed into organised societies whose artistic achievements can be appreciated in the art, ceramics and weavings of the Chavín culture (900 to 500 BC) and in the beautiful pastel shades of the pottery of the Nazca culture which succeeded it. While these occupied central Peru, the powerful Mochica culture was developing on the coastal desert of northern Peru. As well as its expressive pottery graphically illustrating all aspects of human life (including various sexual practices), the Mochica culture displays remarkable achievements in irrigation and building as can be witnessed today in the vast remains of the Mochica city of Chan Chan built of sand and situated outside the present-day city of Trujillo.

Meanwhile there is evidence of developed societies at an even earlier period in central Mexico in the enigmatic Olmec culture of the Gulf coast lowlands (1,500 to 400 BC) with its distinctive carved stone heads. A succession of cultures in central Mexico have left us the ruined temple cities of the Totonacs, the Zapotecs and the Toltecs. Teotihuacán, outside Mexico City, with its huge stone pyramid to rival those of Egypt, is said to have housed some 300,000 people in about 300 AD.

Mayans, Aztecs, Incas

These were but the predecessors to the three great American civilisations which in certain respects reached levels of development which surpassed anything known in Europe at the time of the conquest. The most attractive of these was the Mayan culture which flourished between 300 and 900 AD in the area of southeastern Mexico, Guatemala, Belize and into parts of El Salvador and Honduras. The remarkable stone cities found amid the jungles of the region testify to the high level of cultural achievement reached by these people. Here they developed an arithmetical system more accurate than that in use in Europe at the time. Their books, of which only three survived the zeal of European missionaries who sought to burn them all, testify to astronomical observations and calculations of great complexity. Their complicated hieroglyphics, in which inscriptions are found beautifully carved in great quantity on their temple buildings, and their delicate carvings of figures with their distinctive curved noses testify to a people of high refinement.

While this civilisation was already but a memory when the Spaniards arrived, it was the Aztecs of Mexico and the Incas of Peru whose empires astounded the Europeans. This was true not only of the beautiful gold and silver ornaments which stimulated the conquerers' greed but also of the engineering feats involved in the Aztec capital of Tenochtitlán. With an estimated population of 300,000 at the time it was larger than any contemporary European city with the possible exception of Paris. The Inca empire, larger in extent than anything known in Europe since the time of the Romans, equally impressed the Spaniards with its developed road system over the mountains, its efficient public communications using messengers, the *chaski*, and its public storehouses which were kept full of food for use in time of war or natural disaster. It was claimed that none of the estimated 30 million inhabitants of the empire went hungry whereas in today's Peru, with a population of some 20 million, up to half the population is estimated to be undernourished.

This, then, was the world stumbled upon by small bands of Spanish adventurers in 1492. Yet, trusting in their superior weaponry and their horses which terrified the locals, making the most of the confusion their arrival engendered among the rulers they encountered and winning allies among disaffected subject peoples in both Mexico and Peru, the Spaniards had within a little over 40 years conquered both empires. In August 1521, after a ferocious struggle, Hernán Cortés took possession of Tenochtitlán. Twelve years later in November 1533 the Inca empire fell when, after baptising and then executing the emperor Atahualpa whom he had taken prisoner through abusing his hospitality, Francisco Pizarro captured and pillaged the capital Cuzco.

Part of the weakness of both empires which facilitated relatively easy conquest was their highly centralised power structures. The capture and execution of the emperors in both cases left resistance disorganised and demoralised, though this was more true in the Inca case then in the Aztec. Once in control, the Spaniards quickly consolidated their power by replacing native rulers with Spaniards while initially leaving the basic power structures and landholding systems intact. To give a facade of legality to this situation (something that concerned the conquerers greatly), the Spanish *encomienda* system was extended to America whereby leading soldiers were given jurisdiction over lands and their inhabitants. These latter were then forced to pay tribute and to provide labour.

As the Spaniards consolidated their control over the empires they conquered, they gradually extended their formal hold over most of the continent. By 1550, the Spanish Crown's formal writ extended from present-day California to the south of Chile and Argentina. Apart from a major revolt by the Incas soon after the conquest of Peru, during which a large army besieged Cuzco for ten months and almost retook it, Spanish rule was never seriously threatened. The harsh treatment of native peoples did, however, provoke periodic revolts, the most notable being that of Tupac Amaru in 1780-81. Claiming descent from the Inca emperors, he led an army of 80,000 in a direct challenge to colonial rule. It took two years of brutal repression for the colonial authorities to reassert their control.

Brazil

Meanwhile the Portuguese had begun to exploit Brazilian dyewood following Pedro Álvares Cabral's landing in Brazil in 1500. Six years earlier under the Treaty of Tordesillas in 1494, Pope Alexander VI had created an imaginary line 370 leagues (about 1,400 land miles) to the west of the Azores, granting the Spaniards all land to the west of it, the Portuguese all land to the east. Though its existence was unknown to Europeans at the time, this left them with much of present-day Brazil. In the early decades, Portuguese rule never extended to more than a few coastal settlements, however, and the few native peoples they encountered were at a relatively primitive stage of development. With no stories of fabulous wealth to tempt them further, it was safer not to venture too far inland. It was not until late in the 16th century when the Portuguese began to develop a lucrative sugar growing industry in the northeast of Brazil that effective conquest of the interior of that vast country was begun. This conquest of the interior still continues at the end of the 20th century.

From the beginning very distinct patterns of settlement evolved in Latin America to those which were to evolve in North America, thus laying the foundations for very different societies to emerge. Large plantation agriculture developed throughout Latin America gradually encroaching on the traditional communal lands of the indigenous. Whether growing crops for export, such as sugar and tobacco, or to feed the urban centres, such as wheat and maize, the huge *haciendas* which developed were often too big to exploit efficiently all their land and reduced the lot of their labourers to impoverished dependence. Despite land reform in some countries, the legacy of this landholding system still acts as a major impediment to development in many Latin American countries. In North America, on the other hand, settler families came to work quite small plots of land, ensuring a more efficient use of the land and the development of a relatively prosperous and stable population able to buy the produce of others and stimulate production throughout the economy.

Voices of protest

The first voices raised in protest against the virtual enslavement of the native population in the Spanish colonies were those of a group of Spanish Dominican friars who arrived in Hispaniola in 1510. Shocked by the treatment of the native peoples by the Spaniards who turned a deaf ear to the friars' criticisms, they appealed to the king. This opened a long period of struggle during which the Spanish Crown on a number of occasions sought to enforce certain standards of treatment for the native peoples. While essentially a power struggle between the Crown and the new Spanish ruling class in America, the friars' pleas proved a useful weapon for the Crown in its attempt to reassert its control in the colonies. Disillusioned by their failure to protect the native peoples, some of the friars began to demand more radical measures, including the restitution of the former native rulers.

Perhaps more important than any lasting improvement in the lot of the conquered peoples, the friars recorded the cries of protest of the natives and began a prophetic tradition which has flowered again in our day in liberation theology. The best-known was Bishop Bartolomé de las Casas (1484-1566) who clearly saw and denounced the real motive for the conquest: "Their reason for killing and destroying such an infinite number of souls is that the Christians have an ultimate aim, which is to acquire gold, and to swell themselves with riches in a very brief time and thus rise to high estate disproportionate to their merits."[2] Many of the Dominicans suffered for their defence of the rights of the native peoples. Some were brought before the Inquisition, others deported back to Spain. Antonio de Valdivieso, Bishop of Nicaragua from 1544 to 1550, was stabbed to death on the orders of the powerful Contreras family. As the liberation theologian, Fr Gustavo Gutiérrez says, the Spaniards were thus the only European colonial power to provoke a discussion at the highest levels of the legitimacy of their colonial presence and their methods.

Colonial economies

Under colonial rule, the main economic purpose of Latin America was to enrich Spain and Portugal. Thus the most important activity was exploiting the silver and gold mines which became the principal source of royal revenue. The most important silver mine was that of Potosí in present-day Bolivia. Today a small town at the southern end of the Bolivian altiplano betraying little of its glorious history, it was in the 16th and 17th centuries one of the largest and richest cities in the Western hemisphere. Similarly rich silver mines were developed in Zacatecas and Guanajuato in Mexico while gold was found in central Chile and in the interior of Colombia. Much agriculture, especially the livestock introduced by the Spaniards, was developed to support the mining industry. Other activities, such as sugar growing, were developed to meet demand in the metropolitan country. Products which competed with those of Spain, such as wine or olives, were actively discouraged as was manufacturing. All trade was monopolised by Spain and carried on through a small number of licensed ports.

Brazil's economy soon took on a similar configuration. The development of sugar plantations demanded abundant labour and the shortage of labourers as well as the need for food to ensure their survival stimulated the development of the southern part of the country. This was given over to cattle raising and raids on the indigenous population of present-day Paraguay which provided a source of labour. At the end of the 17th century, rich deposits of gold, silver and diamonds were discovered in central Brazil, in the present-day state of Minas Gerais. Here the city of Ouro Preto (meaning 'black gold') displays in its fine churches and palaces the wealth of colonial Brazil. In its museums can also be seen some of the ways in which the miners tried to keep a little of this wealth for themselves. One memorable exhibit is that of a saint's statue with a hollow inside in which to hide from the sharp eyes of the royal officials a few grains of gold or perhaps a few diamonds.

The reduction of the native populations throughout the Americas from an estimated 100 million to some 10 to 12 million in the first 70 years of the conquest led to the introduction of African slaves in ever growing numbers. By the end of the colonial period, they constituted 12 per cent of the population of Spanish America and 50 per cent of the population of Brazil. Though the treatment of slaves varied from owner to owner, the large numbers of suicides and the low rate of reproduction gives some indication of how terrible was their lot. Slave revolts were not uncommon, particularly in Brazil, and on a number of occasions they managed to establish free settlements some of which lasted for some years before finally succumbing to military expeditions sent against them. The most celebrated of these was the "republic of Palmares" in the northeast of Brazil which held out for most of the 17th century against numerous Portuguese expeditions.

"Triumph of humanity"

A bright spot in this barbarous history of inhumanity was the Jesuit "Reductions" whose existence has been highlighted in the feature film *The Mission*. Often referred to collectively as the Jesuit Republic of Paraguay, these comprised thirty self-governing cities of the native Guaraní people strung along both sides of the Paraná river which today forms the border between eastern Paraguay and northern Argentina. It was the raids by white slave traders from southern Brazil which convinced the Jesuits of the need to establish these cities. They date from the early 17th century when three Jesuits, one of them the Irishman Thomas Field, ventured into the area to work with the Guaraní.

Even today, the ruins of these cities testify to the high level of artistic endeavour achieved there. San Ignacio Miní on the Argentine side of the river had a population of 3,659 in 1733. On one side of the large plaza is the church and adjoining it the residence of the Jesuits, the school, workshops and kitchen. Fanning out on the other three sides are the solid, communal, brick homes of the Guaraní.

Each city was completely under Guaraní rule with two or three

Jesuits living in each. Apart from their religious and educational duties, the Jesuits acted as a last court of appeal when serious disputes arose. Those sentenced, however, were allowed to choose their own punishment. To protect themselves from possible attack from slave traders, each city maintained an army and the Jesuits ensured that the only white person allowed to visit was the local bishop. Some cities supported orchestras as is illustrated in the carved frieze in the ruined church in the city of Trinidad on the Paraguayan side of the border. It is known that orchestras from these cities travelled to Buenos Aires to give concerts. The cities had some of the earliest printing presses in the Americas and published books in Guaraní. The astronomical observatory at San Cosmé was renowned even in Europe. To Voltaire, no great lover of the church, these "Reductions" (from the Spanish title *reducciones* meaning places of education and formation) represented "the triumph of humanity".

It was a triumph that could not last. Angered by the Jesuits' defence of the native people, the colonial authorities finally persuaded Charles III of Spain to expel the Order from his territories in 1767. This opened the way for the break-up of the cities. Their legacy lived on, however, as the absence of a land-holding class in that part of South America made Paraguay the most progressive state in the Americas following its independence in 1811 and today Guaraní is the only native vernacular language of any American state. These ruins stand as a reminder of what might have been had the "encounter of cultures" which began in 1492 led to a real cultural and economic interchange. Instead, the real impact of Europe is summed up in this Mayan lament:

> "It was only because of the mad time, the mad priests, that sadness came among us, that Christianity came among us; for the great Christians came here with the true God; but that was the beginning of our distress, the beginning of the tribute, the beginning of the alms, what made the hidden discord appear,
>
>> the beginning of the fighting with firearms,
>> the beginning of the outrages,
>> the beginning of being stripped of everything,
>> the beginning of slavery for debts,
>> the beginning of the debts bound to the shoulders,
>> the beginning of the constant quarrelling,
>> the beginning of the suffering.
>> It was the beginning of the work of the Spaniards and the priests..." [3]

Footnotes

1. Quoted in Pablo Richard '1492: The Violence of God and the Future of Christianity' in *1492-1992: The Voices of the Victims*, London, SCM, 1990, p 66
2. Quoted in Enrique Dussel, op. cit., p 36
3. Quoted in Pablo Richard, op. cit., p 60

Chapter 3

Independence: Missed Opportunities

"One could argue that these countries [of Latin America] have been independent since the 19th century. There was a decolonisation – purchased with the blood of the poor – but that process was taken over by merchants, generals and landowners. Their appropriation of the continent's independence drove us toward forms of alienation and colonialism which I believe are worse than the ones Latin America endured before its independence."

– Eduardo Galeano, Uruguayan writer and journalist[1]

The independence movements in Latin America are often attributed to the influence of European liberalism and the French Revolution. Much more decisive, however, were the internal divisions within the colonial ruling class in the four viceroyalties into which Spanish America was divided by the end of the 18th century – the Viceroyalty of New Spain covering the region of Mexico and Central America, the Viceroyalty of New Granada covering Colombia, Venezuela and Ecuador, the Viceroyalty of Peru which included Chile and the Viceroyalty of La Plata covering Argentina, Bolivia, Paraguay and Uruguay. Brazil, under Portuguese rule, was also constituted as a viceroyalty. These divisions, between the colonial administrators born in America, the *creoles*, and those who had come from Spain, the *peninsulares*, sowed the seeds of independence. The creoles who had gained more power as a result of lax rule by Spain found themselves losing out to *peninsulares* under the Bourbon reforms of King Charles III (1759-88) who tightened up royal administration of the colonies. Marginalised from the key positions of power in civil society and the Church and confined economically by Spain's monopoly on trade, they were susceptible to the ideas of the Enlightenment and the American Revolution. As the German naturalist and geographer, Alexander von Humboldt reported when he arrived in Latin America in 1799, a common saying among the creoles was: "I am not a Spaniard, I am an American."[2]

Independence struggles

The influence of Enlightenment ideas however did not inspire any concern for the lot of the impoverished masses. Indeed the political struggles which resulted in the independence of almost all of Spanish and Portuguese America between the years 1810 and 1824 were motivated more by a fear of what would happen if the masses revolted and a concern to ensure that this did not happen. The initial phase of the independence struggle in Mexico was an exception as the revolt led by the parish priest of Dolores, Miguel Hidalgo, gathered a disorganised horde of indigenous and mestizos, miners and urban workers, armed with machetes, slings and pikes. Hidalgo, an avid reader of Enlightenment authors, decreed the end of slavery and of the tributes paid by the native peoples, and the return of lands confiscated from the indigenous communities. His revolt, continued after his capture and death by the more organised and in some ways more radical priest, José María Morelos, was eventually defeated. However, Mexican independence, when it finally came in 1821, conformed to the Latin American pattern in that it was led by the army officer who had played a key role in putting down the priests' revolts, Agustín de Iturbide. His firm conservatism was seen by the local creoles as a surer guarantee of their social status than was the link to the rather shaky Spanish monarchy of the time. Iturbide immediately proclaimed himself emperor but his empire lasted only a few months and he was forced to abdicate and go into exile in Britain. When he dared return in 1824 he was captured and shot by troops of the new republican regime.

The creoles throughout the continent were similarly motivated by a desire to maintain their economic and social dominance at all costs. The slave revolt of Toussaint L'Ouverture broke out in Haiti in 1791, defeated an army sent by Napoleon in 1802 and proclaimed Latin America's first independent territory in 1804. This had inspired widespread fear throughout the Americas. In neighbouring Cuba, the lack of enthusiasm for independence among the creole ruling class must have been motivated to some extent by what had happened in Haiti and the island became Spain's last American colony to achieve independence in 1898. Indeed but for the difficulties of the Spanish monarchy in the early decades of the 19th century, independence might not have come as early to most of Latin America. With Spain occupied by Napoleon in 1808 and King Ferdinand VII his effective prisoner, creole leaders took power from royal officials in various Latin American capitals including

Caracas, Buenos Aires, Santiago and Bogotá. Yet their motivation was far from clear and most continued to proclaim loyalty to Spanish rule until the restoration of the king in 1814. His stubborn refusal to make concessions to the liberal demands of the creoles and his determination to restore strict royalist rule was what finally pushed many creoles to opt for independence.

Meanwhile, the difficulties in Spain became the opportunity for the most visionary of the continent's advocates of independence, Simón Bolívar. His military campaigns, begun in Venezuela in 1811, led eventually to the independence of Venezuela, Colombia and Ecuador as the united state of New Granada in 1821. In the south, José de San Martín helped consolidate the independence of Argentina before moving on to liberate Chile (1817) and joined Bolívar to liberate the centre of Spanish rule in South America, Peru (1821). Both leaders were however disillusioned by their achievements. San Martín left for France in 1823 where he died in virtual obscurity in 1850 while Bolívar died on his way into exile in 1830 despairing of achieving the continental unity which had been his dream. Indeed the only two attempts to forge united states out of the multiple administrative units which were the legacy of Spanish rule soon floundered. The state of New Granada only lasted to 1830 while the United Provinces of Central America which won independence in 1821 had by 1823 split into the five republics we know today.

Brazil too benefited from Napoleon. His occupation of Portugal in 1808 forced the royal family to set up court in Brazil and to end the restrictions which had allowed the colony trade only with the mother country. When King João returned to Lisbon in 1820, the creoles feared a loss of their new-found prosperity and prestige and so they persuaded the royal son and heir, Prince Pedro, who had remained behind in Río de Janeiro, to become the first emperor of an independent Brazil in 1822. Foremost among their concerns also was the need to find a road to independence that would not disturb the prevailing social structure as they feared political unrest could spark a revolt by the large black slave population.

Class division intact

Latin American independence therefore left largely intact the division of society between the small ruling class which monopolised wealth and power and the great majority of peasants, indigenous peoples and artisans, many of whom were virtual slaves to their masters. In some ways the lot of the poor majority worsened. Though inadequately enforced, laws had existed under colonial rule to protect the indigenous peoples. With the local landed aristocracy now firmly in power in the new republics, the remaining communal lands of the indigenous proved too tempting for them to resist. As the 19th century progressed, laws were enacted in all the republics which led to the expropriation of these lands. This encroaching capitalist agriculture relegated the indigenous populations to tiny plots on the worst land. Often unable to scrape a living, they ended up as highly exploited labour on the plantations or migrated to cities in search of work. The breakup of Church estates by liberal, anti-clerical governments further exacerbated rural class divisions as in most cases the land was bought up by landlords, either local or foreign, and was rarely divided among small farmers. This trend was further boosted from the 1870s onwards as growing demand in Europe for such export crops as coffee, cotton, sugar, bananas, tobacco and livestock products led to the further consolidation of huge estates.

Meanwhile, the weak manufacturing class of small artisans also suffered as a result of independence. With the ending of the colonial restrictions on trade, Latin American markets were flooded by cheap manufactured products, particularly from Britain, against which local producers could not compete. Though the more enlightened rulers who achieved power in the new states saw the need to stimulate local manufacturing and agriculture and develop a bigger domestic market, such aspirations fell prey to the impact of the international economy and to endemic domestic instability.

Ultimately it was this instability which destroyed the many attempts to develop a more vibrant economy which could benefit larger sections of the population. The ruling elites which took control of the new states were divided between the conservative landed aristocracy allied to the Catholic Church and the more liberal elements of the emerging bourgeoisie with interests in manufacturing and trade and inspired by the modernising ideology of progress through science. In many states, these political differences coincided with a cleavage between those who wanted a strong unitary state (usually the conservatives) and the federalists (usually the liberals).

Though endowed through liberal constitutions with all the paraphernalia of liberal democracies – congress, an independent judiciary, regular elections – these states had won independence through the barrel of a gun. Real political power rested with local *caudillos*, strong leaders whose power depended on superior force rather than democratic legitimacy, though some used this power to modernise the states over which they ruled. The next half-century was dominated by the struggle in almost all Latin American states between the liberals, believing in the rule of law, and the strong-arm *caudillos*. Such instability stymied all attempts to implement coherent programmes of national development.

Paraguay: developing a nation

One country did, however, show the potential for national development that existed. This was Paraguay. It emerged into independence in 1811 through resisting the pressures of the creole authorities in Buenos Aires and under the leadership of the remarkable lawyer, José Gaspar Rodríguez de Francia, who embarked on a policy of isolation and self-sufficiency. This he saw as the only alternative to submission to Buenos Aires which controlled the country's main outlet to the sea down the Paraná River. Under his authoritarian rule, Francia implemented a policy of state-led economic development unique for its time. By breaking up the landed estates and dividing the land among the labourers, he created a stable class of prosperous small farmers. Contrary to what happened elsewhere in Latin America, he recognised the communal lands of the indigenous peoples and respected their Guaraní language. Through a network of state farms, he diversified agriculture replacing export crops such as tobacco and sugar with foodstuffs for domestic consumption. His development of livestock allowed him end a dependence on imports from Argentina. He protected Paraguay's industry from imported goods and stimulated the development of new industries. As two Swiss visitors who stayed in the country from 1819 to 1825 wrote, "the blacksmiths became locksmiths, mechanics and bladesmiths, the shoemakers became saddlers and harness makers, the silversmiths became smelters and the builders became architects."[3] He introduced compulsory education up to the age of 14; by 1860, the country had 435 elementary schools with some 25,000 pupils and the highest literacy rate in Latin America.

When Francia died in 1840, his policies were followed by his successor Carlos Antonio López who benefited from Argentine recognition of his country's independence and opening of the

River Paraná to Paraguayan trade. From 1851 to 1860, the value of Paraguay's exports increased more than five times and were worth more than double its imports. With the help of foreign engineers and other specialists, the land-locked country built the most advanced steam ships in Latin America and while other countries were paying Britain to build railways, the Paraguayan state built the first wide-gauge railway in the River Plate region. As the US historians Benjamin Keen and Mark Wasserman sum up the period: "The relative absence of peonage and feudal survivals contributed to a rapid growth of Paraguayan capitalism and the well-being of its predominantly Indian and mestizo population. When López died in 1862, Paraguay was one of the most progressive and prosperous states in South America."[4]

The good example could not be to allowed last, however. Its neighbouring states found an excuse for war and, with the active support of Britain, an alliance of Brazil, Argentina and Uruguay went to war with Paraguay in 1865. Though the Paraguayans fought tenaciously under Francisco Solano López (son of Carlos Antonio López) and held out against vastly superior numbers for five years, they were finally defeated in 1870 at catastrophic cost. Some three quarters of the adult population of 500,000 was killed and the male population reduced to 30,000. Territory was lost to Argentina and Brazil and a puppet regime installed which undid the progressive achievements of Latin America's first real experiment in economic independence. The country has never recovered.

Growing dependence

If Paraguay developed through keeping foreign penetration at bay, the rest of Latin America found itself burdened with ever greater debts as it came to depend more and more on foreign capital, particularly from Britain. As the century went on so the dependence grew. In 1870, foreign capital was still limited to such areas as trade, shipping, railways and public utilities. By 1914 it had entered the continent's key productive areas – mining, ranching, agricultural plantations and manufacturing. Nowhere is this dependence better illustrated than in the railways built by the British in the second half of the century. In contrast to railways in Europe which link major centres of population to one another, in Latin America most railways run from mines or agricultural plantations to the ports from where the wealth extracted was exported. Accompanying economic dominance came political interference even to the point of encouraging war. One such was the War of the Pacific (1879-83).

In the 1870s British capital funded the exploitation of nitrate deposits by Chilean companies in the Atacama desert where Peru, Bolivia and Chile met. Aggressive tactics by these companies soon led to threats by both Peru and Bolivia to expropriate companies active in their territories. To Britain's obvious interest in the Chilean side was added its hostility to Peru and Bolivia, both of which had suspended repayments on outstanding British loans. When war finally broke out in 1879, two warships Chile had recently acquired from Britain quickly turned the balance in its favour and by January 1881 Lima was in Chilean hands. As a result of the Chilean victory, Bolivia lost its access to the sea and the port of Antofagasta while Peru lost its southern province of Arica. Chile increased its national territory by some one third, gaining in the process full control of the valuable nitrate deposits.

An even more bizarre foreign intervention was the French attempt to establish a Mexican empire under its protection. This attempt, which had the active support of both Britain and Spain, came as liberal forces were gaining the upper hand on the conservatives in 1860. Fearful of liberal dominance and seeking to ensure their loans to Mexico were repaid, the three countries sent in a joint force in January 1862. Britain and Spain soon withdrew leaving Napoleon III to offer the throne of Mexico to an Austrian prince, Archduke Ferdinand Maximilian. During his years in power as Emperor of Mexico (1864-67), France never really subdued the country and the whole attempt came to a sorry end when Maximilian was captured and executed in May 1867.

Era of prosperity

The year 1870 marked a watershed in Latin America's development. The new demands of an expanding Europe for the continent's raw materials, both mineral and agricultural, opened an era of relative prosperity. This benefited both the landed aristocracy and the modernising bourgeoisie, helping both to find a common interest, often in simply enjoying the fruits of their new-found wealth. While much investment went into developing infrastructure in this period, little serious attempt was made to develop an extensive industrial base. Much of the wealth therefore served simply to satisfy the conspicuous consumption that remains a hallmark of the Latin American elite to the present day. More significantly, the republics' economies came to rely for the bulk of their export income on one or two commodities – Brazil on coffee and sugar (and briefly rubber), Chile on copper and nitrates, Peru on guano and, when this ran out, on sugar and silver, Cuba on sugar, Central America on bananas and coffee, Argentina and Uruguay on meat and wheat. In many cases, this dependence endures in a modified form down to the present day. It marked a new form of colonialism which continues to impede the continent's development.

The demand for labour quickly increased in this period. In 1888 Brazil became the last Latin American country to abolish slavery, symbolising the slow emergence of a more modern labour market, though forms of semi-slavery persisted. Peru imported some 100,000 Chinese coolies between 1850 and 1875 whose conditions were little better than those of slaves. The later part of the 19th century also saw countries like Argentina and Chile conquering some of the last independent indigenous peoples of the continent with the effective expansion of these countries to the south. The Mapuché people of southern Chile put up a fierce resistance until their final defeat in 1882. This opened new opportunities for European immigrants who, in the final decades of the century, flooded into Argentina, Uruguay, Chile and Brazil in particular. The population of Buenos Aires grew from 500,000 in 1889 to 1.2 million in 1909. In Chile, German immigrants colonised the south of the country which to this day remains distinctly German. Among the immigrants to Argentina, mostly Spaniards and Italians, were also many Irish. Many of these immigrants joined the small but growing working class from which a trade union movement and left-wing parties began to emerge by the end of the century. In Argentina, anarchism gained many converts among the working class and was a major force for the first two decades of the 20th century.

Uruguay was the country which benefited most from this wave of immigration. It was a favoured destination for left-wing and anarchist dissidents fleeing from Europe. Under the leadership of José Battle y Ordóñez who was president from 1903 to 1907 and again from 1911 to 1915, it became the world's first welfare state. He established the eight-hour working day, old age pensions, minimum wages and accident insurance; he separated Church and state and recognised divorce; he abolished capital punishment and through active state intervention developed the infrastructure on which a prosperous and stable state was built for the next seventy years.

Uruguay was the exception, however. If Latin America entered the 20th century with relative prosperity, this remained concentrated in the hands of a small elite. Both rural and urban poverty remained widespread and in most cases social legislation was only won through harsh struggle. Meanwhile, the United States was beginning to rival British economic dominance. Already in its 1846-48 war with Mexico after which it gained California, New Mexico and Texas (about half the territory of Mexico) and in its toleration of the takeover of Nicaragua by the US adventurer William Walker in 1855, it was showing its inclination towards military intervention in the region. In 1898 it annexed Puerto Rico and won effective control of Cuba after its independence in the same year. The early years of the 20th century were to see its creation of Panama in 1903 and its armed intervention in Central America and the Caribbean. With the 'Roosevelt Corollary' to the Monroe Doctrine, enunciated by President Theodore Roosevelt in 1904, it took upon itself the right to intervene in Latin America at will. It was a right that was to be used a lot throughout the coming century to ensure a compliant continent.

Footnotes

1. Eduardo Galeano in an interview in *Latinamerica Press*, 19 February 1987, p 4
2. Quoted in Benjamin Keen and Mark Wasserman, *A Short History of Latin America*, Boston, Houghton Mifflin, 1980, p 145
3. Juan Rengger and Marcelino Lomgchamp, 'Ensayo historico sobre la revolucion del doctor Francia', Imprenta de Moreau, Paris, 1823, p 74, quoted in Sergio Guerra Vilaboy, *Paraguay: De la independencia a la dominación imperialista 1811-1870*, Havana, Editorial de Ciencias Sociales, 1984, p 75 (translated by PK)
4. Keen and Wasserman, op. cit., p 187

Chapter 4

Nationalism and Populism: Attempting National Development

"If at the end of the Second World War anyone had predicted that within forty years Latin Americans would be selling aircraft to the British Post Office and the Royal Air Force he would hardly have been believed. Yet Embraer of Brazil has done just that."

–Hugh O'Shaughnessy, British journalist[1]

The Mexican Revolution (1910-17) broke unexpectedly on a smug Latin American ruling class which had grown used to the opulent lifestyle it could maintain from the profits of the export-import economy. The relative political stability this prosperity gave Latin American states at the end of the 19th century masked the continuing impoverishment of these countries' masses. Nowhere was this more true than in Mexico where the corrupt and venal dictatorship of Porfirio Díaz (1876-1911) had run the country as the personal fiefdom of the landed aristocracy. The twin revolts of Pancho Villa in the northern border state of Chihuahua and of Emiliano Zapata in the southern state of Morelos in 1910 marked a determined demand by Mexico's landless labourers, small farmers and indigenous peoples for a share of the country's wealth through access to land ownership and secure livelihoods. But alongside this another revolution was taking place as the more liberal sectors of the elite sought to develop democracy as a condition for capitalist development. The subsequent seven years saw these two revolutions struggle for control; the result was a compromise which has conditioned Mexican politics ever since.

This compromise is best expressed in the contrast between the remarkably progressive 1917 Mexican Constitution and the political system which emerged out of the revolution. The Constitution placed severe restrictions on the Catholic Church and these were lifted only at the end of 1991. It also contains an advanced labour code recognising workers' rights, curtails the rights of foreigners to own Mexican property and allows for a far-reaching land reform through the extensive expropriation of large estates. If implemented, these provisions would have delivered a death blow to the landed aristocracy, given the marginalised masses a share in Mexican society and ended foreign control of key economic sectors. In practice most have been implemented only in a limited fashion while a highly centralised and authoritarian political system has managed to contain and co-opt more radical demands.

Import substitution

The Mexican Revolution does, however, contain the seeds of the first real attempt to develop Latin America for the Latin Americans and to give the impoverished masses a share in the benefits of this development. This attempt, which historians now call ISI or import substitution industrialisation, emerged out of a growing recognition that the export-import economy left Latin America completely dependent on the vagaries of international conditions over which it had no control. While these had brought the region a certain prosperity from 1870 onwards, the First World War slowed demand for its raw materials and exposed its dependence on manufactured imports. This spurred attempts to develop a manufacturing base in many Latin American countries though it was not until the Great Depression in 1930, which brought the sudden collapse of the region's export markets, that ISI came to be formulated into a coherent set of policies for national development. While implemented differently in different countries, the nationalist regimes of the populist leaders Getúlio Vargas in Brazil (1930-45; 1950-54), Lázaro Cárdenas in Mexico (1934-40) and Juan Domingo Perón in Argentina (1946-55; 1973-74) are regarded as the fullest political expression of this project.

Even before the Crash of 1929, many Latin American countries faced growing economic difficulties which led to social unrest and political instability. Markets for Chile's primary export, nitrate, collapsed with the discovery of techniques to make chemical fertilisers and it had to rely on copper for the bulk of its export income. Fluctuating international copper prices coupled with growing strikes among the country's nitrate and copper workers led to political instability with the military intervening on a number of occasions in the 1920s and 1930s. While mostly of the right, these governments did include the Socialist Republic of Colonel Marmaduke Grove which lasted from 4-16 July 1932. In El Salvador, the collapse of coffee prices on which the country depended for its income led in January 1932 to a revolt by rural peasants against falling wages and deteriorating living conditions. The newly installed government of General Maximiliano Hernández Martínez unleashed the military on them leading to the deaths of tens of thousands of peasants and indigenous (estimates vary from 10,000 to 45,000). Though not as badly hit by the Great Crash, Argentina too saw the military take power in 1930 fearful that the democratic government of Yrigoyen was going to threaten the interests of the landed elite. This opened what became known as the "infamous decade" of harsh repression and corruption. Within a year of the October 1929 Crash, the military had taken power in Argentina, Brazil, Chile, Peru, Guatemala, El Salvador and Honduras in most cases to safeguard the interests of the elite, a role they were to play with ever greater thoroughness as the century wore on.

Brazil: Getúlio Vargas

The major exception was Brazil where a military revolt in late 1930 paved the way for the accession of Getúlio Vargas to the presidency. Though far from a convinced nationalist when he took power, his long and dictatorial rule (from 1930 to 1945, and again from 1950 to 1954) encouraged the growth of domestic Brazilian industry and set the country on the road to becoming a major world industrial power. This was in part due to the crisis of 1929-30 which saw a collapse in the international price of coffee, Brazil's primary export, but it also owed something to the conditions under which Vargas had won the presidency through the support of nationalist army officers and more radical political leaders. Among these was the young army captain, Luís Carlos Prestes, who had led a revolt of *tenentes* or junior officers in 1924 and whose legendary 14,000 mile march through Brazil convinced them of the need for radical social and economic change. Prestes was later to become leader of Brazil's Communist Party.

In his early years, Vargas relied on some of these *tenentes* who helped him consolidate his power. In this period he introduced major reforms including a liberal electoral code in 1932 and, in 1934, a new constitution giving the state a key role in economic development with specific mention of "the progressive nationalisation" of mines, mineral deposits and essential industries.[2] Under a new industrial tribunal workers won basic rights such as the eight-hour day, fixed minimum wages and an elaborate social security system. His various measures to encourage domestic industry resulted in a doubling of industrial production between 1931 and 1936.

But Vargas soon revealed his true political colours with a lurch to the right and the establishment of a dictatorship under the title *Estado Nôvo* (New State) by 1938. It reflected some of the trappings of European fascism of the period but in practice was much more populist. Though it introduced strict press censorship and a clampdown on all dissent, including a complete ban on strikes, it continued to champion workers' rights albeit through a highly authoritarian and centralised structure. The state took an even more active role in industrial development through economic planning and direct investment in heavy industry such as mining, oil, steel and chemicals. Vargas was able to play on US fears of his sympathy for the Axis powers to gain valuable financial and technical assistance from Washington. This help, the first public US funds allocated to industrialisation anywhere in the Third World, allowed the completion of the huge Volta Redonda steel plant, a cherished dream of Vargas. By 1946 the National Motor Company had been created to manufacture cars and airplane engines, the first step in making Brazil one of the world's largest arms manufacturers. In the crucial strategic area of oil production, Vargas set up a corporation, Petrobras, with a state monopoly on oil production and exploration.

The Vargas era showed some of the essential elements of import substitution industrialisation. It was a state-led effort to manufacture at home products which had previously been imported. Thus it was primarily oriented towards domestic production rather than exporting. The state's involvement was central through tariff barriers, tax incentives, exchange controls, lowered duties on machinery and raw materials for industry as well as through providing direct investment and favouring domestic producers in government contracts. But it was not exclusive; private investment, both domestic and foreign, was also welcomed. In the Brazilian case, the large firms established in heavy industry were mostly joint ventures between state and

44

private investors. Among the enduring results of the ISI therefore was the consolidation of an industrial bourgeoisie, the emergence of a strong urban working class, and the acceleration of migration from the countryside to the cities.

Mexico: Lázaro Cárdenas

In Mexico, Lázaro Cárdenas (1934-40) emerged from within the leadership of the ruling National Revolutionary Party to assume the presidency. Already the gains of the revolution had been largely negated by the conservative and self-serving elites which had dominated power in its aftermath through the ruling party, the only one permitted. Though hand-picked by Elías Calles, the de facto ruler for the previous decade, Cárdenas immediately moved to assert his independence once he assumed office and in 1936 ordered the deportation of Calles to the United States. Consciously modelling himself on the Soviet Union, his election platform included a Six-Year Plan.

This he implemented vigorously, instituting a massive land distribution programme including state support and credit for the new owners. Together with the provision of rural schools, medical centres and much improved roads, the living standards of Mexico's rural poor improved substantially, in the process creating a new domestic market for industry. This he stimulated through protective tariffs and government loans. The *Nacional Financiera*, established in 1934, acted as a national development corporation giving support to domestic industry. The high-point of the Cárdenas presidency, however, was the controversial nationalisation of the oil industry in 1938 when the British and US companies which controlled it ignored a Supreme Court ruling in favour of striking oil workers. The date of the expropriation, 18 March, is still celebrated by Mexicans as their declaration of economic independence and the state oil monopoly, Pemex, is viewed as an untouchable national asset to this day.

Cárdenas maintained the authoritarian power structure he inherited. Under this the ruling party permitted one trade union confederation and one peasant confederation, effectively under party control, which acted as the sole channel for disputes and grievances. Cárdenas did however replace the discredited CROM labour confederation with the *Confederación de Trabajadores Mexicanos* (CTM) which gave active support to strikes and he reorganised the ruling party (re-naming it the Party of the

Mexican Revolution). While his policies won him strong support from labour and the peasantry, he did nothing to lessen the co-option of these sectors by the ruling party for its own ends. His gestures, such as giving firm support to the Republicans in the Spanish Civil War, refusing to recognise the Franco regime when the war ended and offering political dissidents exile in Mexico, the most famous of them Leon Trotsky, infuriated the US and the Mexican right but endeared Cárdenas further to the Mexican masses. His period in office marked the high-point of the attempt to implement the principles of the Mexican revolution.

Argentina: Juan Domingo Perón

It was in Argentina, however, that this nationalist project found its most intense populist expression in the person of Juan Domingo Perón. An army colonel, he emerged onto the political stage as Minister for Labour in the military government which took power in a coup in 1943. For most of the century, Argentine politics had been dominated by the middle class Radical Party which, however, had failed to break Argentina's dependence on the export of wheat and meat products. Industrial development, which was slow, was almost completely in foreign hands. The military leaders who took over in 1943 were intensely nationalist; they aspired to industrialise and modernise Argentina in order to free it not only of its dependence on agricultural exports but also of its foreign domination.

Perón agreed with these aims but his genius lay in recognising the emerging working class as a potential ally in this process. As Minister for Labour he encouraged workers to organise and backed their strikes so that their share of the national income increased by 25 per cent between 1946 and 1950. He also created a state social security system which gave the organised working class not only generous pensions and health benefits but also such privileges as holiday complexes of the type associated with communist countries. This he was able to do due to the large surpluses then being generated by Argentine exports; workers' incomes could grow but not at the expense of profits. Perón soon became the leading figure in the military government and a natural candidate for the presidency in the 1946 election. He resigned from the military, established his own Labour Party and won the presidency comfortably, much to the consternation of Washington which feared his strident rhetoric against Yankee imperialism.

Once in power, he embarked on a massive nationalisation programme, bringing the Central Bank, the railways, the oil industry, insurance, communications, electricity, the airlines and dock facilities into state ownership. Under a five-year plan, labour-intensive industry grew and was further stimulated by the growing buying power of the working class. He established a state monopoly in the export of agricultural goods, buying them at fixed prices and profiting from the buoyant international prices then obtaining. The restive military he kept satisfied with increased salaries and the modern equipment they craved.

In his highly successful attempts to build a mass base of support, Perón's wife, Eva, proved his greatest asset. Ostracised by Buenos Aires high society, she established her own foundation and personally distributed gifts of money and goods to the poor. This earned her a fanatical following and to this day she is viewed by many Argentines, including younger progressive people, as a saint. The combination of the pro-labour Perón and the high-profile charitable activities of 'Evita', consolidated a political movement, based on the organised working class, whom Perón referred to as the *descamisados*, the shirtless ones. Despite the vagueness of its ideology, *Justicialismo*, which promised a third way between capitalism and communism and the movement's at times erratic swings between left and right, Peronism has proved deeply-rooted and continues to dominate Argentine politics.

While his policies seemed remarkably successful during his first years in power, by the early 1950s major problems began to appear as the international prices of Argentina's agricultural exports began to decline. This showed the weakness of import substitution: though substituting consumer imports, it created a deeper dependence on the import of technology which had to be paid for by the export of primary products. Any decline in the international prices for these products caused balance of payments problems at home. This is what hit Perón forcing him to institute more conservative policies, including austerity programmes, and to appeal for foreign investment. Gradually alienating various sectors of his support base, he resorted to repression to contain unrest while his rhetoric grew ever more strident. This culminated in an attack on the Catholic Church in 1954 when he legalised divorce and brought parochial schools under government control. Peronists orchestrated attacks on churches while in response the Vatican excommunicated the entire government including the president. Finally, in 1955, the military stepped in and deposed Perón. He spent most of the rest of his life in exile and was allowed to return to Argentina only in

1973 when he was re-elected president and died in office a year later.

Perhaps the most enduring political legacy of these populist leaders in Latin America's three largest countries is, at a crucial moment of its emergence, to have mobilised the working class into movements that ensured its subservience, while at the same time severely repressing any independent unions or left-wing parties. In Mexico, the alliance between labour and the ruling party (now known as the PRI) still endures; in Brazil, the military governments from 1964-85 built on Vargas' legacy of one confederation effectively under the supervision of the Ministry of Labour; in Argentina, the essentially middle-class Peronist movement has dominated working class politics.

Reform and revolution

A country which could have greatly benefited from the modernisation which these regimes implemented was Peru. The politics of the Peruvian leader, Victor Raúl Haya de la Torre, had proved very influential throughout Latin America. As a student leader, he founded the *Alianza Popular Revolucionaria Americana* (APRA) in 1924 and argued for a pan-Latin American struggle against Yankee imperialism. This must involve the nationalisation of land and industry, the internationalisation of the Panama Canal and solidarity with the oppressed of the world, he wrote. Though establishing a solid working class base of support, Haya de la Torre saw the middle class as "the abused class that will lead the revolution."[3] APRA has dominated Peruvian politics since the mid 1920s but, though it claimed to have won presidential elections on a number of occasions, the military always stepped in to prevent it taking power. It was not to be finally allowed to govern until 1985.

In other countries, however, import substitution policies were implemented in ways that saw the growth of more authentic working class movements. In Chile, where a militant working class had emerged in the bitter strikes of nitrate and copper workers at the turn of the century, the Communist Party, the more moderate Socialist Party and the middle class Radical Party formed a National Front which won the presidency in 1938. This instituted a policy of state-led industrialisation under the state development agency, CORFO, established in 1938. Though it saw a large increase in the numbers of the industrial working class and in their living standards, by the mid-1940s the political tensions proved too much and the Socialists and Communists split from the Radicals. This period did, however, re-inforce the class basis of Chilean politics which was to find dramatic expression in the Salvador Allende government of 1970-73.

In Guatemala, the social democratic regimes of Juan José Arévalo from 1945-50 and of Jacobo Arbenz from 1950-54 sought, in the words of Arbenz "to transform our nation from a backward country and a predominantly feudal economy into a modern capitalist country...economically independent."[4] The agrarian reform of 1952, which broke up large estates and distributed 1.5 million acres to 100,000 peasants, met with the implacable hostility of the US multinational United Fruit Company which had close links with the Eisenhower administration. A CIA-organised coup in 1954 put the landed oligarchy back in power and it has ruled the country since with a brutality shocking even by Latin American standards.

The country which succeeded in implementing the most thorough going revolution in this period was Bolivia. In 1952, the National Revolutionary Movement (MNR) took power, led by Victor Paz Estenssoro and supported by armed indigenous miners and peasants. This implemented a land reform which transferred land ownership from the large landowners to the peasantry and it nationalised the principal source of the country's foreign earnings, the tin mines. These it placed under joint worker-government management, a system which gave remarkable power to the trade union movement. It also abolished the military, organising instead peasant and worker militias. These reforms have in time been undone, partly under intense US pressure and also due to the need for foreign investment to modernise the tin industry. A national army was again established and trained by the United States and since the mid 1960s this acted as the political party of the right, taking power successively to contain the militant workers' movement. Paradoxically, the army was able to return to barracks in the 1980s as the MNR still under Victor Paz Estenssoro (in his 80s) returned to power to undo some of the more important gains of his revolution.

From the 1930s to the 1950s, therefore, Latin America was able to take advantage of the opportunities provided by international events (the 1930s Depression, the Second World War and the Korean War), to begin a process of industrialisation and modernisation. More importantly, it sought to end its dependent position inherited since colonial times and to achieve an economic independence. While this had certain limited success, it created a new form of dependence on imported technology and exposed the limits of any attempt by dependent underdeveloped economies to achieve economic independence. In its creation of strong working class and political movements to mobilise (and control) the workers, in the ever quickening pace of migration to the cities which it stimulated and in the heightened expectations for a share in the national wealth which it created among the marginalised masses, it laid the foundations for the subsequent decades.

Footnotes

1. Hugh O'Shaughnessy, *Latin Americans*, London, BBC Books, 1988, p 134
2. Quoted in Benjamin Keen and Mark Wasserman, *A Short History of Latin America*, Boston, Houghton Mifflin, 1980, p 358
3. Quoted in Thomas E. Skidmore and Peter H. Smith, *Modern Latin America*, Oxford University Press, 1989, p 203
4. Quoted in James Dunkerley *Power in the Isthmus: A Political History of Modern Central America*, London, Verso, 1988, p 115

Chapter 5

Crisis and Repression: The Elites Fight Back

"The possibility of significantly improving the distribution of income by correcting some aspects of the system's functioning, without altering the system itself, is no longer believable after the experience of many attempts at 'reform' in Latin America."

— Gustavo Gutiérrez, Peruvian theologian[1]

By the time the 1960s opened, the promise offered by industrialisation and modernisation was beginning to prove illusory. The region's terms of trade were disimproving as the prices its raw materials fetched on the world market declined relative to the cost of the region's imports. For most commodity products, this decline was to accelerate over the next thirty years. It reduced the income of most governments, leading them to impose austerity policies which hit the working class and the poor hardest. Meanwhile, the nationalism associated with the early phases of industrialisation was giving way to ever greater foreign control as multinational companies set up plants within Latin American countries reducing sections of the native bourgeoisie to a dependent position, often eager to do the bidding of their foreign masters. Furthermore, the attempt to broaden the internal market – through such measures as breaking up the large landed estates and making the tenants into small proprietors or through sharing the benefits of growth with the working class – had floundered. The result was growing political unrest in most countries as workers and the more liberal sections of the bourgeoisie fought back against what they perceived as a growing rightward shift.

The promise of Cuba

The victorious entry of Fidel Castro and his guerrilla army into Havana on 1 January 1959 sent shock waves through Latin America which were to have long-term repercussions. The overthrow of one of the continent's most odious dictatorships, despite its firm backing by the United States, was greeted with rejoicing and gave fresh heart to those groups resisting the imposition of right-wing measures by their own governments. The radicalisation of the Cuban revolution over subsequent years with its extensive land reform, its nationalisation of foreign firms, its success in raising the living standards of the majority and its defiance of Washington inspired a whole generation to believe that capitalism could be overthrown and a socialist utopia established. The failure of ISI to achieve national economic independence and share society's wealth more equitably convinced many that only socialism could achieve these goals.

The 1960s therefore saw the emergence of guerrilla movements in many Latin America countries as a younger generation rebelled against the cautious leadership of the traditional left led by communist parties. Some of these guerrilla groups proved relatively short-lived and constituted no more than a nuisance to governments. Best known was the Bolivian Ñancahuazu movement but only because Ché Guevara left Cuba to join it and his capture and summary execution on 8 October 1967 drew momentary international attention. In Peru, the left-wing of the APRA party broke away in 1959 and by 1965 had set up two rural centres of guerrilla action. The Peruvian armed forces, supplied with napalm and counterinsurgency advice by the US military, had little difficulty in wiping them out. In Brazil, a number of small guerrilla groups staged some spectacular actions including the kidnapping of the US Ambassador in September 1969 but they were soon defeated. In Venezuela where the guerrilla movement of the early 1960s was relatively large, the Communist Party had by 1967 come to realise its futility and re-entered electoral politics. In Mexico, the appearance of rural guerrillas in 1971 shook the ruling establishment which based its legitimacy on the revolution of 1910-17 and which had given strong diplomatic support to Cuba.

Largely led by middle class students and intellectuals, these movements followed a strategy which they derived from the success of the Cuban guerrillas. Known as *foquismo*, it contradicted traditional communist theory by emphasising the role small bands of guerrillas could play in triggering a revolution and in defeating a standing army. These urban students and intellectuals believed the oppressed peasantry would rise up if given the opportunity and that such rural revolt would undermine the power of the state leading to its eventual collapse. It proved a disastrous failure as, ignorant of the conditions of

52

rural life, the guerrillas found themselves unable to communicate with the peasantry who often betrayed them to the military. The lessons of this failure were to be learned in such countries as Guatemala and Nicaragua where a resurgent movement in the 1970s mobilised sectors of the rural population with great success.

In other countries, however, the guerrilla movements of the 1960s had a major impact. In Colombia, a guerrilla war has been going on for over 30 years which the armed forces have been unable to defeat. Four main groups have been active, each in different parts of the country. Among them is the ELN, the group with which the well-known priest Camilo Torres was killed in combat in 1966. The FARC, whose roots pre-date the Cuban revolution, claims 12,000 members while the more populist M-19 gained international attention by such daring attacks as the takeover of Bogotá's Supreme Court building in November 1985 leaving 95 dead. Only in the late 1980s, as successive presidents attempted to draw them into electoral politics, were there signs of some end to this war.

In Argentina and Uruguay, the guerrilla movements of the 1960s were largely urban-based. The Tupamaros in Uruguay and the Montoneros in Argentina raided police stations, robbed banks and kidnapped and killed industrialists, politicians and diplomats. Capitalising on the discontent generated among the working class in both countries by the economic downturn of the 1960s, their activities brought growing panic to sectors of the middle class and to the military.

Alliance for Progress

If the Cuban revolution emboldened the left, it also spurred Washington to act. President Kennedy's accession to power in 1961 coincided with the launch of the Alliance for Progress under which the US would support reformist, civilian governments throughout Latin America. This was designed to counteract left-wing influence through effective economic and social progress. Such civilian governments as those of Jânio Quadros in Brazil (who lasted only seven months in 1961), Rómulo Betancourt in Venezuela (1958-64), Arturo Frondizi in Argentina (1958-62), Alberto Lleras Camargo in Colombia (1958-62), Fernando Belaúnde Terry in Peru (1963-68) and Eduardo Frei in Chile (1964-70) were presented by Washington as models of the new moderate reformism that would bring prosperity to Latin America. The early promise was soon tarnished, however, as some countries lurched to the left before succumbing to military rule with active US support (Brazil and Chile), others succumbing more directly to various shades of military rule (Argentina and Peru) and Colombia, though remaining formally democratic, paralysed by violence. Venezuela alone appeared to progress as Washington might have liked but this was due largely to its huge oil reserves. Meanwhile, the rhetoric of the Alliance for Progress was rudely shattered when President Johnson sent 22,000 marines into the Dominican Republic in 1965 fearing, with little evidence, the emergence of another Cuba there.

The Alliance for Progress, as with the many governments it supported, fell victim to the deep structural problems of the Latin American economies and to the growing political polarisation these were causing. While this led to many right-wing governments, it also led to some genuinely progressive ones, the most important being the Popular Unity government of President Salvador Allende in Chile (1970-73). This sought to deepen the rather cautious reforms of the Frei administration through a land reform that finally expropriated and broke up the large landed estates and through the nationalisation of the copper industry, the country's main foreign exchange earner. Paradoxically, since Allende did not have a majority in Congress he had to rely on existing laws including ones passed by the Frei administration and even ones of the short-lived "Socialist Republic" of 1932. Workers' incomes rose by 50 per cent in the first year, unemployment fell and inflation was kept under control. The hostility of the US which stopped all economic credits and aid (while increasing aid to the Chilean military,) and a fall in international copper prices, began to create problems for Allende in 1972. Meanwhile a fall in food production largely caused by the disruption of the land reform as well as active sabotage by a fearful middle class which reached a climax in the employers' strike of October 1972, fuelled social unrest. As emerged later, this was actively fomented by the United States which spent $8 million between 1970 and 1973 to destabilise the Chilean economy. When Popular Unity increased its vote in mid-term congressional elections in March 1973 from 36 per cent to 44 per cent, serious plotting for a military coup began.

Generals take power

The brutal military takeover in Chile in September 1973 was to prove the norm for Latin American politics in the 1970s. Instead of reformism or revolution, the continent was facing a protracted period of military rule, first signalled by the military coup in Brazil in 1964 which toppled the progressive and pro-labour government of President João Goulart. By the late 1970s every country in mainland Latin America except for Colombia, Venezuela, Mexico and Costa Rica was under military rule. Thus began a most savage attempt to restructure Latin American society, usually known as the national security state.

The roots of the national security state lie in the failures of the project of ISI of the 1930s-50s but also in the Cold War climate which saw in the insurgencies of the 1960s the growing influence of the Soviet Union on the region. The fear of such influence was the overriding strategic concern of the United States and it had dominated post-war relations between Washington and its Latin American allies. The continent's republics pledged in the Rio treaty of 1947 to join the United States in defending the hemisphere and justified military intervention in any country threatened with "communist penetration". This fear was elaborated into the doctrine of national security and inculcated into the region's military elites in the School of the Americas, a US training college in the Panama Canal Zone. By the time it closed in late 1984, some 44,000 Latin American officers had studied there, among them Generals Augusto Pinochet of Chile, Alfredo Stroessner of Paraguay, Anastasio Somoza of Nicaragua, Hugo Banzer of Bolivia and Leopoldo Galtieri of Argentina, all of whom later became dictators of their countries. Such courses greatly professionalised the Latin American military but also created a deep dependence on the United States, re-inforced by annual meetings with US military chiefs. Following the Cuban revolution, training in counterinsurgency including the torture techniques which were to be widely used throughout the region, became a feature of these courses. This, the more sinister underside of the Alliance for Progress, was hidden from the US public.

As much as a desire to combat internal unrest, the military took power in the 1960s and 1970s with a firm and even enthusiastic belief that only through liberalising their economies, inviting in foreign (largely US) capital and ending state intervention in economic life could real economic development take place. But if the state was to withdraw from economic life, it was to keep an iron grip on political and social life, suppressing all dissent and allowing only such political life as it controlled. In some cases, notably Argentina and Chile, the military sought to abolish all politics, blaming politicians for the ills of the nation and putting their trust in so-called apolitical technocrats.

Brazil: the first national security state

Brazil, where the military ruled from 1964-85, led the way. The first national security state, it also acted as the laboratory in which the model was elaborated. One of the first acts of the military was to give foreign companies advantages over domestic ones with reduced taxes, easier access to credit and special exchange rate privileges (though later phases of military rule facilitated an enhanced role for domestic industry in conjunction with the state). Meanwhile wages were frozen, strikes banned and unions taken over by the military. To maintain a facade of democracy political life was re-organised with two approved parties, the pro-military ARENA and the catch-all opposition, the MDB. Critics and dissidents were purged from politics, academic life and the media. As the years went on, the military's grip tightened and by the end of the 1960s torture was being routinely used.

The results were predictable. Foreign capital flooded in leading to a virtual takeover of Brazilian industry, whole sectors of which went bankrupt. Though industry grew, it was largely concentrated in the south-east of the country (particularly in the São Paulo region) thus further accentuating the inequalities within the country. With the military's firm hold on wages and trade unions, workers' incomes fell so that by 1976 their real purchasing power was reliably estimated to have fallen back to 1962 levels. Meanwhile huge profits were being made, most of which were repatriated. While total foreign investment from 1964-71 was $670 million (over half of it from the United States), remittances abroad in the same period reached $2,319 million. Following the 1973 recession, however, when foreign investment fell, the state became more actively involved in industrial development and the growth of such key sectors as the arms and the computer industry has happened largely under domestic ownership. The regime's 1969 land reform which promised to divide unused land among the landless, proved in practice merely a means of modernising agriculture leading to the development of agribusiness by local entrepreneurs or by multinational companies. The result was to drive more peasants from the land into the cities. Meanwhile, the country's foreign debt grew alarmingly as governments borrowed to cover a growing trade deficit and to modernise the country's infrastructure.

No one doubts that Brazil went through an economic miracle in the late 1960s and early 1970s but it was a miracle that enriched foreign multinationals and their Brazilian collaborators while the majority of the population got poorer and poorer. Brazil is today the capitalist world's seventh or eighth most powerful economy and one of the world's largest food exporters with more land under cultivation than the United States. Yet it has the sixth largest number of undernourished people in the world with malnourishment responsible for seven out of every 10 deaths among children under five years of age. According to World Bank estimates, some 70 million Brazilians out of a population of some 150 million, are poor. That is the contradiction of the "Brazilian miracle".

If Brazil led the way, its example was followed by Bolivia in 1971, Chile and Uruguay in 1973 and Argentina in 1976. The main difference was that, learning from their Brazilian counterparts, these imposed more savage repression from the beginning and dispensed with even the facade of democracy. Under these regimes, "to disappear" became an active verb as thousands of people were picked up by the military never to be seen again. The number in Argentina is estimated at up to 30,000 between 1976 and 1980, most of them people with no history of political involvement. The full extent of the repression in Chile did not surface until the report of the Rettig Commission was published in 1991. This documented the cases of 2,279 victims who were disappeared, executed or who died under torture while over 1 million people out of a population of some 12 million are estimated to have been displaced under the military, either internally or as exiles abroad.

"Military socialism"

While the military regimes of the right gained most international attention, the late 1960s and 1970s also saw a number of military regimes of the left take power in Latin America. Most notable among these was the regime of General Juan Velasco which took power in 1968 in Peru, a country whose development and modernisation had been continuously impeded by the military throughout the 20th century. General Velasco proclaimed a nationalist revolution "to wrest Peru from its apathy and backwardness...to modify radically the traditional structures of our society...to confront those who uphold the status quo."[2] He moved decisively to implement a thoroughgoing land reform, to nationalise the oil and mining industry and to give workers a share in the ownership and management of industry. Diversifying its former dependence on the United States it opened trade with the socialist bloc. While gaining the firm support of much of the Peruvian and Latin American left, the attempt at "military socialism" as it was often called ran into difficulties due to its inherently authoritarian nature. Seeking to mobilise workers and shanty-town dwellers, the regime could also show a repressive side when these showed too much independence. What slowed the tide of reform and eventually reversed it was the international recession of 1973-74; by 1975 General Velasco had handed over power to the more right-wing General Morales Bermúdez who showed less enthusiasm for radical reform.

Other progressive military regimes of this period included those of General Omar Torrijos in Panama (1968-78), General J.J. Torres in Bolivia (1970-71) and General Guillermo Rodriguez Lara in Ecuador (1972-76). What characterised all these was a strongly nationalist outlook expressed in an attempt to modernise their economies under national control. These regimes are a reminder of the long tradition of nationalism within the Latin American military often associated with leaders who have experienced at first-hand the poverty in which the masses of their fellow countrywomen and men live. This tradition has, however, been weakened by the post-war influence of the United States on the military of Latin America.

Even the economic and social successes of the progressive military regimes proved relatively short-lived. All were followed by more right-wing governments which, if they did not undo all the reforms, undermined state industry through chronic underinvestment and weakened the agricultural sector of smallholders or co-operatives through lack of credits and state support. This was true in particular of the civilian Belaúnde Terry adminstration (1980-85) which marked a return to democracy in Peru. In their long-term results, therefore, the military regimes of the 1970s left similar legacies. While they deepened the process of industrialisation and modernisation, they did so through heavy foreign borrowing which in most cases hid their countries' economic vulnerability. Nor were these legacies unique to countries which had been under military rule; Venezuela and Mexico also became deeply indebted in this period.

In many countries, domestic industry built up between the 1930s and the 1960s was largely destroyed, unable to compete with the inroads of foreign multinationals. Those sectors of the workforce in these new industries became relatively privileged (though still very poorly paid) while large sectors, including migrants from the countryside, languished on the margins of the economy eking out a subsistence living. Many of the improved social benefits and services which these sectors had gained in earlier decades were lost as military governments neglected them in favour of investment in prestige projects. As the military regimes began to hand over power from the late 1970s, therefore, the incoming civilian governments were burdened with huge foreign debts, growing social problems and economies ever more dependent on foreign investment and technology. They were to prove all too vulnerable to the world recession of the early 1980s which plunged Latin America into what is generally recognised as the region's worst economic crisis ever.

Catholic militancy

Other legacies of military rule were more surprising. Most notable among these was the emergence of sectors of the Catholic Church, formerly the most solid and sterile pillar of the establishment, as a vigorous popular movement, mobilising opposition to authoritarian regimes and insistently urging deep structural reforms to create more egalitarian and democratic societies. The seeds of this had been sown from the early 1960s in the work of a new generation of young theologians (later known as liberation theologians) and given authoritative backing by the general conference of Latin American bishops in Medellín, Colombia, in 1968.

As military regimes closed down all avenues for popular organisation and expression of dissent, Church groups took on a new and vital role in many countries, offering space and protection for people to meet and discuss while many Church leaders voiced the critique of government actions which it would have been too dangerous for others to do. In this, the Brazilian Church led the way; its prophetic voice denouncing the abuses of the dictatorship and documenting the impact of government policies on the poor and marginalised, severely undermined the regime's legitimacy.

While this prophetic denunciation, taken up by bishops and whole hierarchies in other Latin American countries, gained most public attention, perhaps more significant was the new model of Church being born in the quiet work of priests and sisters living in shanty towns alongside the poor and helping organise them through basic christian communities to defend their interests. Favoured by Pope Paul VI (who died in 1978), these new forms of Church life have been increasingly put on the defensive under Pope John Paul II who has shown himself less than sympathetic to them, particularly in his appointment of conservatives as bishops.

Basic christian communities are only one of the many forms through which the poor and marginalised began to fashion their own movements for change and at times for simple survival amidst the social crisis of the 1970s and 1980s. Loosely known as the *movimiento popular*, these are everything from soup kitchens to women's clubs, from co-operatives to neighbourhood assemblies, from drama groups to alternative media. They have become the vehicle through which the poor educate and mobilise one another and in some countries they have become powerful actors on the national political stage through their ability to mobilise large numbers of people

Lost decade

Despite the enthusiasm with which the return of democracy was greeted in country after country in the early 1980s, it is now generally recognised as a lost decade for Latin America. Crippling foreign debts coupled with falling prices for most of the region's exports have resulted in sluggish or negative growth rates, deepening poverty, cutbacks in social services and, in some cases, historically high inflation rates (in some cases thousands of per cent). Faced with creditors interested in ensuring their debts were repaid at all costs, most Latin American countries were forced throughout the 1980s to implement drastic austerity and adjustment programmes dictated by the IMF which, as the Inter-American Development Bank put it in its 1990 annual report, "have unquestionably exacerbated the problems of poverty."[3]

In this period, Latin America has become a net exporter of capital to the developed world, receiving $300.5 billion in loans and financing while paying back $472.3 billion, a net transfer of $172.8 billion or $1.46 for every $1 received. Yet, despite paying back such large amounts at the expense of their own development and especially the living standards of their poor majorities, Latin American countries ended the decade more heavily indebted than they began it. The region's debt increased from $242.7 billion to $434.1 billion over the decade. While most of the money borrowed throughout the 1980s went to maintain repayments on existing debt, it is also recognised that little of the original sums borrowed were put to uses that could be called truly developmental. Some was spent on prestige projects but substantial amounts were also creamed off in capital flight by the rich and deposited in foreign bank accounts. In the case of Brazil, the economist Dr Marcos Arruda estimates that

$43 billion, 38 per cent of the country's foreign debt, ended up in such accounts.

Despite such economic and social strains, democratic governments survived throughout Latin America in the 1980s. Except for Haiti, only two coups took place during the decade and both were generals replacing military colleagues: General Efrain Ríos Montt in Guatemala in 1982 and the 1989 coup which removed the region's longest-standing dictator, General Alfredo Stroessner, from power in Paraguay after 35 years. In the latter case the coup leader, General Andrés Rodriguez, quickly called elections and had himself conferred with democratic legitimacy. Even countries long in the grip of the military such as Guatemala, saw one elected civilian president handing power to another when Jorge Serrano Elias took over from Vinicio Cerezo in early 1991. Peru, experiencing the region's most acute insurgency problem and plagued by seemingly intractable economic problems, surprised the world in 1990 by electing the unknown Alberto Fujimori as president over the favourite, world-renowned novelist Mario Vargas Llosa. Fujimori took over from Alan García, becoming Peru's third elected civilian president since the military returned to barracks in 1980. Chile became the last mainland country to return to democracy (apart from Paraguay) when the Christian Democrat Patricio Aylwin took power from General Pinochet in March 1990.

Yet the power of these elected governments remains circumscribed by the military whom many commentators believe prefer to wield it out of the public gaze. Being formally answerable to civilian governments has not hampered the Peruvian or Salvadorean military in carrying out their counterinsurgency campaigns nor has it heightened their respect for human rights. In Argentina, the military finally forced President Carlos Menem to pardon even the few senior officers serving sentences in luxurious surroundings for their part in the "dirty war" of 1976-80.

New challenges

The new civilian governments therefore are showing themselves to be relatively moderate and conciliatory, not just to the military but to foreign financiers, industrialists and governments from whom they hope to get urgently needed investment. Neo-liberal in economic outlook, they are obediently implementing austerity programmes, privatising state industries, laying off public workers and increasing prices for essential utilities, all seen as essential steps to economic efficiency. The one government which took a more radical line was the Alan García administration in Peru (1985-90). It broke off links with the IMF and unilaterally limited its debt repayments to 10 per cent of the value of its exports. As a result of its actions, it was almost entirely cut off from international credit and, far from fulfilling the radical promises which brought him to power in 1985, Alan García left power with the country's economy in shambles and over half its population hungry. This will give pause to any other governments who might contemplate similar moves. Where others have had to limit debt repayments, they have done so quietly, pleading inability to pay.

Meanwhile, the Malvinas war between Argentina and Britain in 1982 which led to the collapse of the Argentine military dictatorship, has had longer-term regional results. Elites throughout Latin America, for long schooled to believe US promises of support against enemies from outside the hemisphere, were shocked by Washington's support for London in the war. This has caused a certain re-assessment of their political dependence on the United States and a return to a more nationalist outlook. This was expressed by such regional initiatives in the 1980s as the Cartagena grouping which sought unified action on the international debt and the Contadora initiative which stood up to Washington on Central America. While the Cartagena initiative floundered as creditors proved adept at implementing a policy of divide and conquer, the Contadora process has led to the establishment of the Rio Group comprising all the countries of Latin America and the Caribbean which co-ordinates positions on a range of issues.

Drugs became another subject of major concern in the 1980s with the US declaring war on the production and processing of cocaine in Peru, Bolivia and Colombia. Stimulated by demand in the United States and Europe, cocaine had become a major industry particularly in Bolivia where President Jaimé Paz Zamora claimed in 1990 that 70 per cent of his country's real GDP was cocaine-related. In Colombia an increasingly embattled government declared war on the powerful drugs barons in August 1989 following a spate of assassinations of leading figures. While rejecting some heavy-handed US moves to eliminate the coca crop from which the drug is made and to interdict supplies, a "drugs summit" between President George Bush and the presidents of Colombia, Peru and Bolivia in February 1990 signalled growing co-operation between the four countries. Another casualty of the US preoccupation with drugs was the Panamanian dictator, General Manuel Noriega, a former CIA informant. The US invasion of Panama in December 1989 won widespread support both in Panama and the US but left economic stagnation in its wake and uncertainty about the number of casualties with the US Southern Command estimating 300 dead but Panamanian human rights groups claiming a death toll of 4,000 to 5,000.

Central America: between suffering and hope

The region which suffered most throughout the 1980s, however, was Central America. The victory of the Sandinista guerrillas in Nicaragua in July 1979 emboldened both the Salvadorean and Guatemalan guerrillas who confidently predicted victory before long. In the case of El Salvador, this may well have happened but for the election of Ronald Reagan as US President in November 1980. Immediately upon taking office the following January, he made El Salvador the first target of his crusade to stop what he saw as the inroads of communism in the region thus delaying for a further decade any attempt to resolve the conflict and its deep-rooted social causes.

Meanwhile the Nicaraguan revolution raised hopes throughout the region that the country could chart a new path towards development. Following more moderate policies than had Cuba, the Sandinista leadership pledged itself to a mixed economy, political pluralism and a non-aligned foreign policy. In the early years, modest growth rates were achieved and living standards rose but the experiment was soon undermined by implacable hostility from the Reagan administration which waged an unrelenting war both through isolating Nicaragua economically and through establishing and financing the Contra rebels.

The US invasion of Grenada in 1983 led many Sandinista supporters to fear a similar fate would befall Nicaragua and, without strong opposition within the US and among its European allies, such may well have happened. Politically isolated from its Central American neighbours and economically cut off from a key trading partner, the United States, the economy virtually collapsed, with more and more of its meagre resources going to finance the war. By 1990 inflation was running at 13,000 per cent and the foreign debt was twenty-seven times the country's export earnings. It was against this background that the Sandinistas were defeated by the UNO coalition under Mrs

Violeta Chamorro in the 1990 elections though they remained the largest single party with some 40 per cent of the vote.

In El Salvador, the growing realisation that the military could never defeat the FMLN guerrillas coupled with a more moderate policy by the Bush administration and vigorous diplomacy by the then UN Secretary General, Javier Pérez de Cuéllar, led to the launching of a series of peace talks under UN auspices. These held out the first real hope for an end to the decade-long war which had made El Salvador dependent on huge injections of US aid to survive. A peace agreement between the government and the FMLN was finally signed in January 1992 with the promise that the security forces will be reformed and the FMLN integrated into civilian political life. With all the five Central American republics ruled by elected conservative presidents, moves were underway towards greater regional integration through rebuilding the Central American common market which had collapsed in the late 1970s, through a Central American parliament and through diversifying the region's traditional exports.

The period 1960-90 may have been marked in Latin America by events which caught the world's imagination such as the Cuban, Chilean and Nicaraguan revolutions, the brutal repression of the region's military dictatorships or the Guatemalan and especially the Salvadorean guerrilla struggles. But the region discovered no new model of development during the period that proved capable of implementing sustained development for the good of the masses. While the United States can be justifiably blamed for undermining the Chilean and Nicaraguan experiments, there is also much evidence that points to severe internal weaknesses in both. Cuba which had raised the living standards of its people dramatically though at the cost of a highly centralised and even repressive political system, ends the period in a major crisis following the collapse of communism in Eastern Europe. Elsewhere, the period ends with most people poorer than they were 20 or even 30 years before, national industry severely weakened and under the crippling burden of massive debts. The tasks facing the new generation of rulers are greater than ever.

Footnotes

1. Gustavo Gutiérrez, *The Power of the Poor in History*, London, SCM Press, 1983, p 117
2. Quoted in *Latinamerica Press*, 6 March 1986, p 3
3. "Latin American poverty 'deepened' by reforms", *The Financial Times*, 8 April 1991, p 5. The IADB does, however, go on to say that despite its short-term costs, a policy of economic reform is the best hope for medium to long-term growth.

Chapter 6

Prospects for Latin America

"We have arrived at the most important crossroads. I consider the 1990s an extraordinarily crucial decade. We are in a time of profound reflection, a time of analysis and thoughtful conversation. We need to analyse both the errors and idealism of the past. This reflection, however, must be accompanied by action to confront as never before the threat (North against South and capital against labour) that is destroying our people.

We need a socialism from the South, without dependence on European socialism, which in my experience was never authentic. There now exists the possibility for a new left in Latin America – democratic, popular and participatory – that destroys the totalitarian and vertical nature of the traditional left."

– Xavier Gorostiaga, Nicaraguan economist and Jesuit priest[1]

The end of the Cold War opens new prospects for Latin America. Since the Second World War, Washington's heavy hand has been active in the internal politics of almost all Latin American countries shoring up the right and seeking to undermine and marginalise the left. With the collapse of the 'communist threat' which Washington used to justify its actions, such overt interference is going to be much more difficult in the years ahead. This is particularly true since the peaceful transfer of power from the Sandinistas to Mrs Chamorro in April 1990 proved wrong Washington's long-repeated dictum that revolutionary regimes would never peacefully hand over power and that covert means to subvert even democratically elected governments were therefore justified. Though Washington may claim in its defence that continuous US pressure on the Sandinistas was what indirectly caused their defeat, such justifications are going to be increasingly hard to sell to the US electorate in the post-Cold War world. The Bush administration's more low-key policy on Latin America with its support for a negotiated settlement to the Salvadorean civil war and its emphasis on economic development throughout the region, is a welcome reversal of Reagan's belligerence. This is not to say that Washington could not find another pretext to justify the use of force; the 1989 invasion of Panama served notice that stopping the drugs trade and its supporters may be one such. Despite this, however, the end of the Cold War opens new possibilities for political forces to emerge that might more effectively and more accurately represent the aspirations of the majority of Latin Americans.

The Latin American left is also undergoing a profound reassessment. The glamour and even mystique often associated with armed struggle and revolution in the past has been largely replaced by a more sober consideration of the demands of building an enduring base of popular support and the possibilities for social and economic change. This coincides with a shift in power within the left away from the more extremist movements associated with armed struggle towards more moderate groups firmly committed to parliamentary democracy. It is to this shift that Jorge G. Casteñeda, Professor of Political Science in the National Autonomous University of Mexico, is referring when he writes: "The very idea of an overall alternative of any sort to the status quo has been severely questioned. It is now practically impossible for the left to think outside of the existing parameters of present-day Latin American reality. Moreover, the idea of revolution itself, central to Latin American radical thought for decades, has lost its meaning."[2]

Guerrilla wars

This assessment is borne out by the negotiations which, in late 1991, appeared to be bringing two of the region's most intractable guerrilla wars, in El Salvador and Colombia, to a final end. The Salvadorean peace talks offered the prospect of significant institutional reform, particularly of the security forces notorious for their human rights violations. Such reforms would not only bring peace to a long-suffering population but also open the political system to various left-wing parties which in the late 1970s and early 1980s had been driven to armed struggle by the brutal intransigence of the right. What remains to be seen is how willing the oligarchy and the military will be in practice to share power with the left and whether the peace accord provides a mechanism for addressing the deep-rooted social inequalities which lie at the heart of the Salvadorean problem.

In Colombia, the left represented mainly by the former guerrillas, the M-19, emerged as a major political force in a constituent assembly entrusted with writing a new constitution that was completed in July 1991. The guerrillas' decision to enter electoral politics has effectively ended the stranglehold of the two main parties, the Liberals and Conservatives. Though other groups, notably the ELN and a section of the FARC, continue the guerrilla struggle, the more the left are seen to survive and succeed in the political arena, the more likely are the guerrillas to follow their example.

In Peru, on the other hand, the brutal guerrilla campaign of Sendero Luminoso and its extension over more and more of the country since it first began in 1980 marks the emergence of a new and more frightening form of guerrilla struggle. Unlike other Latin American guerrilla movements which sought to build a base of popular support among the poor, such as its rival MRTA in Peru, Sendero often resorts to terror tactics to intimidate the rural population to carry out its commands. Motivated by a rigid ideology and deeply authoritarian in outlook, Sendero seeks to extirpate capitalism in Peru as a prelude to a world revolution and thus often takes as its particular target social projects aiming to better the lot of the poor. Dismissed by Peruvians and particularly by the parliamentary left in the early 1980s as a band of adventurers, the country has watched with a growing sense of powerlessness the advance of this hidden enemy within. The Peruvian left regards Sendero as a group of dangerous terrorists which has done immense damage to the poor of the country and which, if it ever came to power, would instigate a reign of terror similar to that of Pol Pot in Cambodia in 1975-78. Already, due to the activities of Sendero and the equally terrorist counter-insurgency campaign of the armed forces, Peru has become a land of daily violence and death and, according to the UN, has every year since 1987 been the country with the greatest number of disappearances in the world. Castañeda writes that Sendero Luminoso "may well be the last revolutionary organisation to survive in Latin America, largely because its isolation from the rest of the hemisphere makes it relatively impervious to the disappearance of the revolutionary paradigm and the corollary notion of permanence."[3]

New politics

In other countries the emergence of new political forces is offering some grounds for hope that a new politics may emerge. In Brazil, the candidate of the Workers Party (PT), Luis Inacio da Silva, known as Lula, surprised all observers by coming second in the country's first presidential election for almost three decades in December 1989. The PT has emerged as Brazil's first left-wing party with mass support having grown out of the popular movement, in particular the basic christian communities, during the military dictatorship. With social democratic, Marxist-Leninist, Trotskyist and other tendencies organised within it, it is the first grass-roots party to break the hold of the wealthy elite on Brazilian politics and, though experiencing many internal tensions, has shown the possibilities that exist for a mass political party articulating the needs of the poor majority.

Even more amazing was the election of Fr Jean-Bertrand Aristide as president of Haiti in December 1990 with 67 per cent of the vote while his nearest rival managed a mere 15 per cent. Again, he had emerged from the popular movement which had grown up under the Duvalier dictatorship and found his support base in it. His sudden overthrow in a coup seven months after he took office came as a surprise as it was thought his widespread international support, including that of the Bush administration, would stay the hand of the military. Yet, even if the efforts of the Organisation of American States (OAS) do not succeed in reinstating Aristide in power, his election has itself been a lesson to the poor of their potential political power. The firm international action against the coup will also make the right realise they cannot continue ruling Haiti as if it were their personal fiefdom. The overthrow of Fr Aristide may show the difficulties facing the new left but it does not negate its emergence as a political force.

Another surprising example of the emergence of a new politics is in Mexico which has effectively been a one-party dictatorship under the Institutional Revolutionary Party (PRI) since 1917 (though the party has gone through a number of name changes in that period). In the July 1988 presidential elections, the left-wing candidate Cuauhtémoc Cárdenas of the National Democratic Front won 31 per cent of the vote while Carlos Salinas, the PRI's candidate, was elected president with only 50.36 per cent, the party's lowest vote ever. Moreover, evidence emerged of widespread fraud by the ruling party prompting many to believe Cárdenas had won a far higher vote. The son of former president Lázaro Cárdenas (1934-40) (see Chapter 4), his split with the ruling party in 1987 catalysed a fragmented left-wing opposition with strong roots in the popular movement. The promise of the 1988 elections, however, was not sustained in mid-term congressional and local elections in August 1991 when the PRI regained many of the seats it had lost to the left. It remains to be seen whether the PRI has successfully regained its hegemony or whether its success in the 1991 elections, due to a large extent to the promise of economic progress held out as a result of the free-trade pact being negotiated with the United States, will prove temporary.

There are therefore certain similarities among the new political forces emerging. They incarnate a new indigenous left, more pragmatic in its politics but with a broad-based support which the traditional left has often lacked. No longer does it offer a seemingly instant, painless solution to national ills but it does promise a management of the nation's affairs that will seek to benefit the poor and marginalised. It envisages the state playing a key role in partnership with the private sector in modernising and developing the economy. It resists the wholesale privatisation so beloved of the neo-liberal governments it opposes but it does admit the need for selective privatisation. It identifies the foreign debt as the greatest obstacle to development and proposes a negotiated limitation of repayments. In Brazil for example, the Workers Party proposed a detailed inventory of the country's foreign debt to show how much of it was actually used for the purpose of national development. The party said that this was the only amount for which any incoming Workers Party government would be morally responsible.

Economic reforms

Paradoxically, it is the liberal governments currently ruling Latin America which claim to offer the definitive solutions to the region's ills which was what the left used to claim. Through the neo-liberal 'shock' austerity programmes, these governments claim to be able to eliminate inflation and through massive privatisation, to liberate enterprise. These packages, agreed with the International Monetary Fund, are also said to be the prerequisite for heavy foreign investment. In some countries, most notably Mexico and Chile, these policies have resulted in a return to sustained economic growth that encourages others to follow the same road. But the cost has been enormous as the growth is achieved by depressing wages to lure in multinational companies, encouraging agribusiness to boost agricultural exports at the expense of growing food to feed the local population, and cutting back on social spending to achieve balanced budgets and curb inflation. It is no accident that the two great success stories of neo-liberal economics in Latin America were the two most authoritarian of the region's larger countries throughout the 1980s. For others such as Brazil, Argentina or Peru, where the conditions did not exist for implementing the neo-liberal package as effectively, economic decline has continued despite the best attempts of their governments. The comment of the historian Edwin Williamson that the Brazilian armed forces had led their country "to a situation where economic progress had become the enemy of social order" could be aptly applied to the region as a whole in the early 1990s.[4]

In highlighting the enormous difficulties that Latin America faces in a world economy in which it is ever more marginalised, the left is being more honest. Despite the region's worsening terms of trade with prices for its principal exports falling relative to the prices it must pay for its imports, many countries managed to achieve healthy export surpluses during much of the 1980s. This they did often by diverting goods from domestic consumption and curtailing imports, at enormous social cost. Yet all these surpluses went to pay interest on the region's foreign debt; a commercial surplus of $28 billion in 1989 only serviced 73 per cent of Latin America's debt. As the region's debt continues to rise, moves by the creditor countries to recognise the seriousness of the problem are still sluggish. The US, in the Brady Plan, has recognised the need for debt reduction and President Bush, in his Enterprise for the Americas proposal, has promised mechanisms to help reduce the debt. Yet, these are still far too modest to make a real difference to most Latin American countries.

Though many countries have had a certain success in boosting non-traditional exports, most are still dependent on one product for a large percentage of export income: Mexico, Venezuela, Ecuador and Trinidad and Tobago on oil, Colombia, Costa Rica, El Salvador, Guatemala, Haiti and Honduras on coffee, Chile on copper and the Dominican Republic and Guyana on sugar. A decade of economic crisis has severely hit investment in infrastructure further setting back prospects for economic growth. And, particularly with eastern Europe providing far more attractive prospects, foreign investment in the region remains sluggish. So sombre are some observers about the region's economic future that they use the term "Africanisation" to describe the growing stagnation and decay they forsee for much of Latin America as it falls ever further behind the world's most expanding economies.

Some hope that new moves for greater economic integration both within the region and between Latin America and the United States will prevent marginalisation from the world economy. Mercosur, a fledgling Southern Cone common market between Brazil, Argentina, Uruguay and Paraguay, has already led to agreement between the four on common taxes, customs policies, international bank rates and stable exchange rates. Moves are afoot to revamp the Andean Pact and the Central American common market while Chile is negotiating a free trade pact with the United States. Even more ambitious is the prospect of a North American free trade zone as Mexico is currently negotiating with the United States to join the zone which also includes Canada. President Bush in his Enterprise for the Americas initiative in June 1990 held out the prospect of a wider free trade zone comprising all of the Americas.

Reaction to these moves has been mixed. While the region's elites by and large welcome the prospect of free access to the huge US market, fears have also been voiced that free trade between the relatively weak and underdeveloped Latin American economies and the United States will prove disastrous to the former. It raises fears of the final destruction of the region's native industry, so painstakingly built up, and it opens the way for the takeover of the Latin American financial and services sector by US companies thus further decapitalising the region's economies. Yet, despite these fears, few see any alternatives as countries which fail to integrate into a continental trading bloc risk being left out in the cold in the new economic world order.

Another trend to be mentioned is the growing trading links between countries of the South. While still a very small percentage of the region's trade as compared with its traditional trade with North America and Europe, these South-South links have been growing and offer potential for a more diversified world trading environment.

European Community

The European Community has also become a significant actor on the Latin American stage during the 1980s. Within the San José process, begun under the Irish Presidency in 1984, EC and Central American foreign ministers meet once a year and a co-operation agreement has been signed between the EC and the Central American common market. To this was added a formal dialogue with the Rio Group, including all the Latin American and Caribbean countries, which since December 1990 acts as a forum for discussing not only issues of mutual concern but also a wide range of international issues. An Irish diplomat involved in these talks, Mr Philip McDonagh, describes them as a "dialogue of equals"[5] and adds that by allowing a certain freedom of conscience and expression on both sides "we Europeans as well as others may have something to learn."[6] An example of this is the acknowledgement of "a spirit of joint responsibility" between debtors and creditors to resolve the problem of foreign indebtedness agreed by both sides at their April 1991 meeting.[7] Also significant is the acknowledgment, in the communiqué following the 1991 EC ministers' meeting with their Central American counterparts, of the seriousness of the region's debt problems and the importance of programmes to alleviate the social effects of economic adjustment. Overall, the involvement of the European Community is important as it acts as a counterbalance to excessive US influence, particularly in the Central American region. This is particularly obvious in the priority it gives to protecting human rights and in its emphasis on fostering internal reforms as a means of resolving the region's problems. The involvement of the Community has added impetus to regional integration, both political and economic, particularly in Central America. As Mr McDonagh put it: "There can be no doubt that as regards regional integration, Latin America is following in the Community's footsteps."[8]

Democracy: enfranchising the poor

None of these factors offer Latin America any guarantee of development. Yet, economic efficiency, regional integration, action to alleviate the debt burden and closer EC involvement in the region's affairs put in place some of the necessary preconditions for such development in today's international environment. Whether they can be used to promote a model of development offering a better livelihood and social benefits for the majority of Latin Americans or whether they do in fact become mechanisms for even greater foreign exploitation may well depend on the governments who will steer the region through the coming challenges.

In this regard, the political history of the region, with its many and unpredictable changes of government and erratic swings in policy may not offer great hope. If there are signs of a new politics emerging with its roots in the popular movement, there is no guarantee this will get to power or, if it does, that it will remain there for long. The emergence of a strong popular movement, already referred to, does in effect, however, act to enfranchise in a politically conscious way sectors of the population which previously were easily manipulated. A dramatic example of this was the rejection by the Peruvian electorate of Mario Vargas Llosa in the 1990 election, despite his sophisticated media campaign, in favour of Alberto Fujimori seen by many as an outsider like themselves. The paradox of this is that Fujimori has ended up implementing the very policies espoused by Vargas Llosa. It is also these politically conscious poor who elected Fr Aristide in Haiti, who almost elected Lula in Brazil and who shook the Mexican political establishment by the vote they gave to Cuauhtémoc Cárdenas in 1988. In Nicaragua also, such voters made up a large section of the 40 per cent of the electorate who continued to support the Sandinistas in the 1990 election despite the mess the country was in. While all these can be interpreted as signs of hope, there is also an element of growing desperation among the poor of Latin America as their situation gets worse and worse. As they totter ever more on the brink, it is survival rather than ideology that governs their choices.

While the poor constitute an unpredictable new element in the electoral arithmetic of Latin America, some sectors of the region's poor masses have learned new forms of self-reliance and solidarity through the popular movement. Survival amidst the economic chaos of the 1980s has for many depended upon an ingenuity, creativity and resourcefulness which would be the envy of many successful entrepreneurs. Indeed some liberal theorists have seen in this "informal sector" the seeds of a popular capitalism taking root. This is to impose categories on the phenomenon which fail to do it justice. Indeed, it has the potential far more to become a popular socialism as it is a process through which the marginalised empower themselves and seek a share in the wealth of their societies through their own organisation. However, while this has been true of sectors of the popular movement, increasingly the harsh struggle for day-to-day survival reduces many to the basic tasks of putting some food on the family table. Where the popular movement can be seen to be having an influence is in the growing awareness among Latin Americans that greater emphasis will have to be placed in future on satisfying basic needs rather than in sacrificing all for the sake of exports as happens too often at present.

Marginalised women are perhaps the greatest beneficiaries of this process. Where the feminist movement has in the North been a largely middle class affair, in Latin America the women's movement has by and large grown out of the popular movement. Marginalised women are often to the forefront of local organisations, of protests, of political struggle though in many cases without seeing themselves as a distinctively women's movement in the way that has happened in the developed world. It was a saddle-maker's daughter who had migrated from the impoverished northeast of Brazil, Luiza Erundina de Souza, who was elected mayor of São Paulo for the Workers Party in 1988, a powerful position as head of South America's largest city and the centre of Brazilian industry. The Latin American women's agenda is far more a social one than in the North, therefore, though it is also changing sexist roles through its attack on traditional Latin *machismo*.

Reassessment

The early 1990s is a time of profound reflection throughout Latin America. The economic crisis of the 1980s, the acute social problems suffered by so many coupled with the collapse of communism in Eastern Europe, the defeat of the Sandinistas in Nicaragua and the crisis of the Cuban experiment have opened a major self-critique among progressive groups about goals and the means to achieve them. This promises to find in the region's own resources new paths towards development with particular emphasis on links with other underdeveloped regions of the world. Already, as a result of the critique of traditional left-wing models imported from Europe, more emphasis is being placed on the new forms of social organisation through which Latin Americans survived the political ravages of the 1970s and the economic ravages of the 1980s. The affirmation of Latin American identity is also leading many to look back again at its indigenous past and the achievements of the region's peoples before the coming of the European conquerers. As the Peruvian anthropologist Rodrigo Montoya has written: "Ours was not an empty continent. Great advances had been made in agriculture, water systems and earthquake resistant construction, for example. Here, the Inca overcame hunger, at the same historical time when hundreds of thousands of people died from starvation in Europe ... America gave to Spain and the rest of Europe, the potato, corn, tomatoes, gold, silver and the idea of a just society in which people do not die of hunger."[9]

The idea of a just society in which people do not die of hunger remains a profound aspiration throughout Latin America. If it has not been achieved, it is not through want of trying as is testified to by a seemingly irrepressible urge which reappears again and again in every era of the continent's history. And that history has, over the centuries, come to include as actors ever wider sectors of the Latin American people. In recent decades, the masses have decisively entered the political stage as actors and not, as in the developed North, as consumers or passive onlookers. But the outlook appears ever more uncertain for them as much of the region languishes in deep economic and social crisis. Whether the resourcefulness of the masses can be mobilised to help find a resolution of this crisis that will benefit them or whether the crisis will continue to exact a heavy toll on them looks set to dominate the next decade.

Footnotes

1. Xavier Gorostiaga in an interview in *Latinamerica Press*, 19 July 1990, p 7
2. Jorge G. Castañeda, 'Latin America and the End of the Cold War' in *World Policy Journal*, Vol VII, No 3, summer 1990, p 478
3. Ibid., p 479
4. Edwin Williamson, *The Penguin History of Latin America*, London, Allen Lane, 1992, p 435
5. Philip McDonagh, 'Reflections on European Political Co-operation', a paper given at a conference on Neutrality and European Political Co-operation in Dublin, 7 May 1991, p 16
6. Ibid., p 20
7. Conclusions of the first Institutionalised Ministerial Meeting between the European Community and the Rio Group held in Luxembourg, 26-7 April 1991
8. Philip McDonagh, op. cit., p 21
9. Rodrigo Montoya, 'Latin America: 500 years of conquest' in *Latinamerica Press*, 26 April 1990.

Part Two

Ireland and Latin America

"A stranger and unknown, I take the liberty of addressing you. I am encouraged to do so by my respect for your high character and by my attachment to the sacred cause which your talents, valour and virtue have gloriously sustained – I mean the cause of Liberty and national independence."

– Daniel O'Connell in a letter to Simón Bolívar, 1820[1]

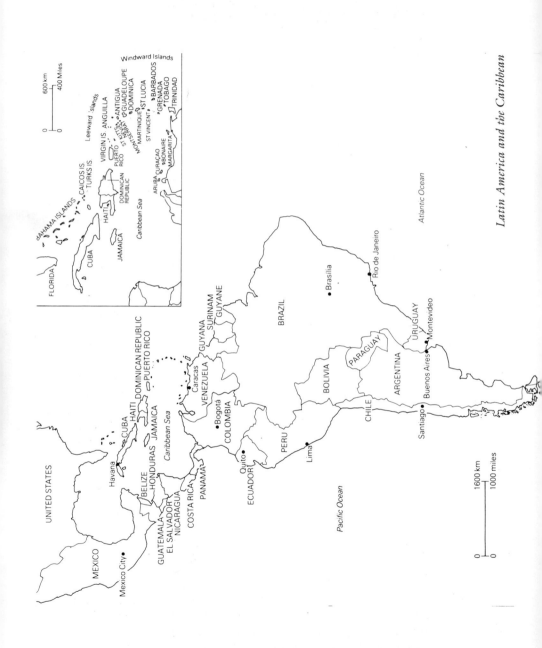

Latin America and the Caribbean

Chapter 7

The Irish in Latin American History: 16th to 18th Centuries

"The historic links in recent centuries of Ireland and Irish immigrants with all of the countries of the New World – of North and South America and the Caribbean – have been particularly close."

– Noel Dorr, Irish Ambassador to the UN, 1980-83[2]

The story of the role played by Irish people at certain periods of Latin American history is a fascinating one. In two parts of the region, Irish immigration resulted in recognisable Irish communities – on the Caribbean islands of St Christopher (today's St Kitts) and Montserrat in the 17th century and in Argentina in the 19th century. Apart from this, many Irish people had an involvement in different Latin American countries, at times playing an important role, most notably in the wars of independence. The O'Higgins family in Chile and Peru can justifiably claim to be the first Irish-American political family while the oldest Irish newspaper published outside Ireland is *The Southern Cross* of Buenos Aires, founded in 1875. Irishmen founded the navies of Argentina, Uruguay and Ecuador while they were among the founders of the Chilean and Brazilian navies. And most colourful of all was the Irishwoman who became first lady of Paraguay during the most crucial period of its history, the War of the Triple Alliance.

St Brendan the Navigator and other early links

Ireland's links with the region begin even before the European conquest however. In their search for the origins of the expectations surrounding the Aztec deity Quetzalcoatl, some Mexican scholars have mentioned the possibility that St Brendan the Navigator (c.484-580) landed on the shores of present-day Mexico. While no hard evidence can be produced to substantiate this theory, Quetzalcoatl was identified as a fair-skinned and bearded figure who had visited the region and promised to return. This was widely believed at the time of the Spanish conquest and was used by the conquerers to their advantage. The hypothesis of a visit by the Kerryman is at least a plausible explanation. Samborombón Bay and River in Argentina are said to be named after him.

There is a similar lack of historical evidence for the belief that Christopher Columbus visited Galway on one of his voyages west and prayed in the church of St Nicholas there. However, there is historical evidence for an earlier visit to Galway by Columbus, probably in 1477. Historians also speculate that there may have been Irishmen among some of the earliest Spanish expeditions, but the brothers Juan and Tomás Farrel, members of the expedition led by Pedro de Mendoza which arrived in the River Plate in 1536 and founded the city of Buenos Aires, are the first recognisable Irish names to be found. While little is known about them, they are thought to have been Irish.

There is also an Irish link with some of the earliest European contacts with Brazil. The first European that we know landed on its shores was the Portuguese, Pedro Álvares Cabral in April 1500 and the Portuguese soon began the commercial exploitation of brazilwood from which the country got its name. We know that the earliest mention of a consignment of the wood reaching Britain came from an Irish port, though the port is not known. This was the 80 pounds which landed in Bristol on 6 October 1503 while a further consignment landed in the same port on 3 January 1504 also from Ireland. Dr David Quinn speculates that these came from either Wexford or Waterford and that the wood had been imported to Ireland from either Portugal or Spain.

An early victim to the Inquisition in Mexico in the 16th century was an Irishman, John Martin. He sailed to the West Indies with the English slave-trader, John Hawkins, in 1567 but was eventually captured by the Spanish and brought before the Inquisition. He claimed to have been brought up a Catholic in Cork but at a young age had gone with his mother to England where they had become Anglicans. Under torture he claimed to have remained a Catholic at heart all his life but admitted to having taken part in what to his examiners were heretical practices. This was enough to have him condemned to be garrotted and his body burned and he was handed over to the secular power to carry out the sentence on 6 March 1575.

Fr Thomas Field and the Jesuit Reductions in Paraguay

The first Irish person to leave his mark in Latin America was the Limerick man, Thomas Field. Born in 1547, he entered the Jesuits in Rome in 1574 and landed in Brazil on 31 December 1577 where he spent ten years as a scholastic at Piratininga, today's São Paulo. During that time he often accompanied the man known as the Apostle of Brazil, the Venerable José de Anchieta, on his missionary journeys. But Thomas Field's real achievements were to be not in Brazil but in Paraguay where he moved in 1587. Indeed he was lucky to arrive at all as his ship was boarded by English pirates in the River Plate estuary and towed out to sea with only five barrels of water on board. He eventually arrived in Asunción with two other Jesuits, Fr Ortega from Portugal and Fr Saloni from Italy, to establish a Paraguayan province of the Society. It comprised not only the territory of present-day Paraguay, but also Uruguay, most of Argentina and central Bolivia, a vast territory as yet virtually uncharted by Europeans. Over the next ten years, Field got to know the Guaraní people through his missionary travels and his recommendations about their evangelisation were to have a major influence on the setting up of the Jesuit "Reductions" (see Chapter 2). These people were numerous and receptive to Christianity, he wrote, and urged that more permanent settlements be established among them. Following an internal dispute about whether the Jesuits should abandon Paraguay altogether due to lack of personnel, he was the only one to stay on in Asunción and attend the key synod of 1603 which, in effect, made the decisions which led directly to setting up the Reductions. The Guaraní were to be evangelised in their own language and be gathered into settlements for their protection against the Spanish and Portuguese slave traders, the synod decided. It also laid down laws protecting the indigenous peoples and condemning, for example, the forced separation of married couples, compulsory marriage or the forcible removal of girls from their guardians. Though we do not know how active a role Fr Field played in these decisions, they do bear the stamp of his approach towards the missionary task. He died in Asunción in 1626 and is credited by the Irish Jesuit historian, Fr Aubrey Gwynn, with being the first Irishman to say Mass in the Americas.

Irish Jesuits

Thomas Field was followed to Latin America by a succession of Irish Jesuits. Indeed, Fr Gwynn points out that of the early Irish Jesuits (from the end of the 16th century to the end of the 18th century) who worked in places outside Europe, the great majority went to Latin America. Altogether up to 26 Irish Jesuits worked in the region during that period. Michael Wadding, born in Waterford in 1586, was the only contemporary of Thomas Field. He entered the Jesuits in Spain in 1609 and moved to Mexico the following year where he worked as a missionary in the remote province of Sinaloa from 1619 to 1626. Between then and his death in 1644, he was rector of Jesuit colleges in Puebla, Mexico City, Oaxaca and Guatemala.

In Mexico, following in the footsteps of Fr Wadding were Fr John Vasquez from Limerick (1631-?), Fr Stephen Font from Galway (1631-73), Fr Cornelius Mac Giolla Riabhaigh from Clare (1635-71), Fr John Muñoz de Burgos, which may represent the names Mooney and Burke (1645-1700), Br Thomas Arsdekin from Waterford (1721-67) and Fr Arsdekin, born in Mexico (1743-88). Fr Thomas Butler from Waterford (1722-90), who was ordained a priest in Mexico in 1749, spent most of his working life as a teacher in Havana, Cuba.

Three Irish Jesuits followed the example of Fr Thomas Field and worked in the Paraguayan Reductions. These were Fr Thomas Browne of Waterford (1656-1717), Br William Leny of Dublin (1692-c1760) and Fr Thaddeus Enis who was working in the Reductions at the time of the Jesuit expulsion in 1767. He died in Spain two years later. Br Andrew Stritch arrived in Paraguay as the Jesuits were being expelled and was deported to Italy where he died in 1773. Doubts exist about the nationality of Br Thomas William Browne who was working in the Jesuit college at Tucuman in 1767. He is described as being English but the Irish Jesuit historian, Fr John MacErlean believes he may have been Irish.

The first Irishman to follow Fr Thomas Field to Brazil was Fr Richard Cary or Carew of Waterford (1619-96). He spent much of his life as a theology professor in Portugal but visited Brazil from 1659-62. Interestingly, unlike most of those who left Ireland at that time, he returned to his native land in 1668 and died in Waterford in 1696. Br Ruperto de Campos (probably a translation of Robert Field) entered the Jesuits in Brazil in 1662 and taught there until his death in Rio de Janeiro in 1712. Fr Thomas Lynch of Galway (1685-1761) rose to become provincial of Brazil from 1750 to 1754 and was expelled with the rest of his fellow Jesuits from Portuguese territories in 1759. Br William Lynch, probably a relation, suffered a similar fate.

Nuevo Reino comprised the present-day countries of Colombia, Ecuador and Venezuela. The first Irish Jesuit to work in this area was Fr Francis Lea of Waterford (1605-75). He was followed by the Galwayman, Fr Ruperto de Acuña, probably Robert Kyne (1620-75) and by Br Thomas Lewis of Drogheda (1648-1721). Three Irish-born Jesuits and two born in Spain of Irish parents worked in Peru. Br Ignatius Walter was born in Ireland in 1625 and joined the Jesuits in Lima in 1669. He died in a Jesuit college in the Peruvian capital in 1672. Br Maurice Ophelan of Waterford (1693-1772) also joined in Lima and had to leave Latin America with the expulsion of the Jesuits from Spain's colonies in 1767. Fr Michael Lynch was born of Irish parents in Seville in 1701 and joined the Jesuits in Peru in 1724. At the time of the Jesuits' expulsion he was rector of the Jesuit college in La Paz in present-day Bolivia. Fr John Brand of Dublin (1712-62) worked among the indigenous of Peru while Fr James Woulfe (1724-83), born of Irish parents in Spain, was working in the Peruvian city of Arequipa when expelled.

Apart from these early Irish missionary endeavours in Latin America, a request was made to Pope Urban VIII by a Spanish Franciscan, Fr Alonso Bonavides, in February 1634 for a mission of Irish priests to go to New Mexico. He was fearful that the English and the Dutch would introduce heresy to that remote northern part of Spain's colonial possessions and wanted priests who could speak English to work not only to protect the native peoples from this heresy but also to seek to convert the heretics themselves! The request, it appears, was never answered.

Irish settlers on the Amazon

Meanwhile the first Irish settlement in Latin America was established on the Amazon sometime around 1612 by an Irish trader, Philip Purcell. He seems to have been of Anglo-Irish stock, from Munster, and was trading out of Dartmouth when he heard of the Amazon while trading for tobacco in Trinidad in 1609. He returned three years later with fourteen Irish, among them a James Purcell, probably his brother. They established an Irish settlement at Tauregue on the mouth of the Amazon close to the present-day town of Mazagao Velho, in an area where there were also some English and Dutch settlements. The Irish seem to have had particularly close links with the Dutch on whose ships they sent their cargoes to Europe.

What attracted all of these to the region were the huge profits to be made from trade in tobacco, dyes and hardwoods. Tobacco from the Amazon was particularly sought after, fetching 30/- to 40/- a lb in England as compared to tobacco from Virginia which sold at only 1/- to 2/- a lb. Dyes and hardwoods of a sort unobtainable elsewhere also fetched high prices in England and Holland. The Irish in particular established good relations with the local Tupi, Carib and Arawak peoples whom they encouraged to expand their tobacco plantations and to supply them with dyes and hardwoods. Later reports indicate that many Irish became proficient in the local languages. The interest for the locals was in gaining European allies against the Portuguese who were beginning to make inroads into the region. Furthermore, they were able to supply these traders with their needs without disrupting their own cycles of planting and harvesting. The arrangement was mutually beneficial and, for the Europeans, yielded instant and sizable profits.

The success of these early settlements encouraged others to follow. A second group of Irish went out in 1620 as part of a larger English expedition led by Captain Roger North. The Irish were led by Bernard O'Brien, a relation of the Earl of Thomond who has left us a colourful account of his exploits. He says his group of twelve Irish and four English "who were servants to the Irish", all Catholics, put ashore down river of the Irish at Tauregue, at a place O'Brien calls Cocodivae close to the present-day city of Macapa. Writing of his group in the third person, he says: "They established good relations with them [the local Indian people], explaining themselves at first by signs until they came to understand the language, which they themselves call Arrua." Despite this friendship, O'Brien says the Irish built themselves "a wooden and earthen fort, surrounding it with a ditch, and for its defence he [O'Brien] had 40 muskets with powder and munitions and other weapons."

The local Indians, he writes, "have continual quarrels and wars amongst themselves" and he obviously took advantage of these to win friends for the Irish. "Going out sometimes to help the Indians of his plantation and district, [he] gained the victory for them with muskets and strategy, and by this won them to his side, and obliged them to cultivate tobacco and cotton for him, and to give him the food and drink of that country." As well as helping them in war, however, the Irish "resolved to bring the

Ireland and Latin America

knowledge of God to the Indians, who had no religion nor did they worship anything as a god or idol. The christians persuaded more than 2,000 of them that there was a God, paradise with relief from care, and a hell with torments after life," he writes.

Though O'Brien obviously inflates the role he played in the expedition, many of the details can be verified from other sources, thus giving the account a certain credibility. Among the more fascinating details is his account of a trip up the Amazon (at this time still largely uncharted) with fifty armed Indians as guides and interpreters. During this journey he made contact with the legendary tribe of women warriors, the Amazons. He writes of reaching a "country where they saw no men but many women, which the Indians call Cuna Atenarea, which means masculine women, to the christians – Amazons. These have very small right breasts like men, [treated] by arts so that they do not grow, in order to shoot arrows, and the left breasts are as large as other women's. They are armed like the Indians. Their queen, who is called Cuna Muchu, which means great woman or lady, was at that time on an island in the river." O'Brien, never daunted, sent her a mirror and a Dutch linen shirt as gifts and in this way got an invitation to meet her. He describes how he had "her dressed in the Dutch linen shirt, of which she was very proud, and at the end of a week, when he took his leave promising to return, she and her subjects signified that they were grieved by his departure."

From 1620 25 these Irish, English and Dutch were at the peak of their prosperity. One account tells of 250-400 settlers of these three nationalities altogether in the area. The English and Irish successfully resisted attempts by the Amazon Company, then being established in London, to bring them under its control. Instead, the Irish seem to have found the Dutch more reliable partners and in 1624-25 a Dutch squadron arrived which, according to some accounts, brought more Irish. These may have been brought out by Philip Purcell who had returned to Europe with Roger North in 1621. Some accounts say that he went further upriver with the Dutch and established a joint Irish-Dutch settlement at Mandiutuba. Relations between the various Irish settlements were obviously good since Bernard O'Brien when he returned to Europe in 1625 left the command of his plantation to Philip Purcell.

Already, however, the Portuguese were beginning to move against the settlers, worried by their incursions in the region which gave the English and Dutch states a certain foothold there. In 1623 a Portuguese force attacked some English settlements forcing their inhabitants to flee to the Irish for protection. The Irish, English and Dutch then united and fought off the Portuguese force. They returned, however, two years later and routed the Dutch and Irish at Mandiutuba, killing Philip Purcell. Another account tells of 70 Irish surrendering to the Portuguese who then massacred 54 of them; these may have been the Irish settlers at Tauregue since O'Brien's settlement at Cocodivae appears not to have been attacked. This effectively brought an end to this phase of settlement but did not mark the final end of Irish efforts in the region.

Two Irish landlords, Daniel Gookin of Carrigaline, Co Cork, and Edward Blennerhasset of Ulster, were associated with attempts in England to establish the Guiana Company in 1629 following the collapse of the Amazon Company, as a means of more official English settlement. Both Gookin, who had already transported 40 Irish from his estate to Virginia in 1622, and Blennerhasset planned to carry other Irish emigrants to the Amazon but these plans never materialised. Meanwhile, some of the Irish captured by the Portuguese in 1625 had secured release through the intercession of the Capuchin Fathers; of these James Purcell and Matthew More returned to England through Spain in 1628. They seem, however, to have had more faith in the plans of the Dutch West India Company to re-establish a colony on the Amazon. They arrived in Holland in September and were soon joined by Bernard O'Brien. Purcell was given command of a group of Irish, Dutch, English and French who returned to the Amazon in April 1629 though O'Brien states that the Dutch made him "captain-general, merchant, pilot, and interpreter" for the colony. Other Irish on this trip included a Matthew O'Malley (who may be the Matthew More released by the Portuguese in 1627) and perhaps William Gayner, an Irishman who had also been on the Amazon and married a Dutch woman. The Dutch also promised to bring more Irish each year. The Irish re-established their settlement at Tauregue. This they reinforced sufficiently to beat off a Portuguese attack the following month but the attackers returned in September in greater numbers. Seeing their situation was hopeless, the Irish seem to have tried to persuade the Portuguese that as fellow Catholics they should be well-treated, stalling for time in the hope of reinforcements arriving. They soon were forced to surrender, however, and were taken prisoner.

These misfortunes did not deter some of the Irish from efforts to return. We find William Gayner back in England in 1633 in contact with the Guiana Company though it was with the Dutch that he returned to the region in 1634, this time to Trinidad. Other Irish seem to have concluded that their best hope of return lay with the Spanish and at least two, Jaspar Chillan and Bernard O'Brien, sought to persuade the Spanish Crown to take a new colony of Irish Catholics to the Amazon. They argued that the Irish were the most appropriate for the task: they knew the local languages and had established good relations with the local peoples whose trust they had won. The Portuguese, on the other hand, had treated the local peoples with brutality. The Irish therefore, argued these adventurers, were more likely to be able to bring the Indian peoples to Christianity. Jaspar Chillan, an Irish merchant resident in Spain whom Fr Aubrey Gwynn thinks was probably a Jaspar Collins from Youghal, Co Cork, made his request to Philip IV in 1631, reinforced by the arrival in the Spanish court at the time of some of the Irish who had been taken prisoner by the Portuguese in 1625 and 1629. The fact that Chillan would have to rely on English and Dutch ships to transport his colony, however, turned the Spanish against the venture since they feared it would facilitate the "heretics" to also gain a foothold.

Bernard O'Brien had already returned to Maránhao, an inland state in the north-east of Brazil then ruled by Holland, in 1634 and been captured by the Dutch authorities as he returned with a local Indian chief. He made his request to the Spanish Crown in 1636 claiming that the Guiana Company had commissioned him to raise 150 Irish soldiers and that they planned to send out 400 Irish men and women whom they would reinforce over subsequent years with Irish settlers from the West Indies. The claim seems exaggerated, however, and the Spaniards must have thought so as nothing came of it.[3]

More successful, at least initially, was the request to King João IV of Portugal by Captain Peter Sweetman around 1643 to transfer Irish from the Caribbean island of St Christopher to the Amazon. This was granted by João IV in September 1643 but never acted upon. In response to another request, the Portuguese king specified in March 1644 that 130 Irish from St Christopher could be settled, half near the city of Belém on the mouth of the Amazon and half in a new town to be built inland. When his council of overseas affairs, the Conselho Ultramarinho, objected that this would unsettle the natives and allow the heretics to make inroads, the king specified that only Irish could partake in the settlement. However, this again does not seem to have been acted upon and in 1646 an identical grant was made to an Irish captain called William Brun or Brum. It is yet possible that evidence may come to light that some Irish settlement did take place as a result of these grants.

Irish emigration to St Christopher and Montserrat

These grants draw attention to the Irish settlement on St Christopher which dates back almost to the beginning of the island's colonial possession by Captain Thomas Warner in 1624. Soon afterwards Anthony Hilton landed on the island and on his way home to England visited Ireland where he awakened interest in settling there. On his return he took a group of Irish people who established a separate Irish settlement. These began growing tobacco but were soon attacked by the local Indians and were forced to move to the English settlement for safety. A document in the Vatican archives dated 1638 from Archbishop Malachy O'Queely of Tuam mentions a request he received for priests to minister to these Irish. He sent two priests with a group of 600 Irish who sailed for the island in March 1638 and these reported they found 3,000 Irish on St Christopher and neighbouring islands. The English Civil War of 1641 is reported to have caused great tension on the island and it is as a result of this that Captain Peter Sweetman made his request to King João of Portugal to move some of the Irish to the Amazon. This may also indicate that some of the Irish who were in the earlier Amazon settlements had ended up on St Christopher and were keen to return. In 1643 an Irish Jesuit, Fr O'Hartegan, wrote from France to the Jesuit superior general referring to a report by a French admiral of 20,000 Irish on St Christopher who were looking for priests who could speak French, English and Irish since "all three are commonly spoken in these parts."[4] Fr O'Hartegan volunteered to go but instead Fr John Stritch SJ from Limerick was sent in 1650. He reported 3,000 Irish each on St Christopher and on Montserrat.

The smaller island of Montserrat appears to have been settled predominantly by Irish people from its first plantation between 1631 and 1634 by Anthony Briskett whose father seems to have been a settler in Wexford. The English Jesuit, Fr Andrew White who visited the island in 1634 reported "a noble plantation of Irish Catholics" there.[5] One report in 1668 says the island was then "almost wholly possessed by Irish."[6] Some governors including Briskett and Colonel William Stapleton (1668-71) were Irish. The Irish influence is testified to by the fact that two of its towns today are called Kinsale and St Patrick's while the shamrock stands as an equal symbol on Government House with the Union Jack. Those who settled on St Christopher and Montserrat seem to have come mainly from the west and south of Ireland, especially Galway and Cork. This may indicate direct trade between these ports and the West Indies. And it appears they maintained a strong sense of identity there as from 1666 to 1668, the Irish on the two islands combined with the French to keep the English forces out.

The Irish legacy is very real for the Montserrat poet, E.A. Markham. During his term as writer-in-residence at the University of Ulster at Coleraine in 1991 he gave an interview reflecting on it. "In the 1630s the Irish came to Montserrat. It was your first and only colony. There is a certain symmetry in my coming to Ireland 300 years later. After all, the first foreign voices I ever heard were Irish, and there are towns with Irish names all over Montserrat. The African slaves took on their master's name, so most black people in Montserrat have Irish surnames, like Ryan or Harris." The Irish presence was seen by the blacks as beneficial, says Markham. "We had the sense that there were different sorts of whiteness, and that white power wasn't the unified monolithic power that it appears to most black people. It was discovered that you could play the English and the Irish off each other and if you were clever you could find an ally in one side or the other."[7]

Cromwellian deportation to the West Indies

Apart from this voluntary Irish settlement, forced deportation became common from 1648 under the English Puritan leader, Oliver Cromwell, who set out to pacify Ireland by force. A Franciscan document dated 1651 tells of 96 priests being held in Carrickfergus ready to be sent as slaves to Jamaica though it appears they were never sent. From 1654 we have a report of an order to deport 59 people from the village of Lackagh in Kildare, including three priests, to Barbados or "other English Plantation Islands in America."[8] In 1655 Cromwell wrote to his son, Henry, requesting 1,500 soldiers as planters for Jamaica. He asks him furthermore to secure 1,000 Irish girls by force and 1,500 to 2,000 Irish boys of 12 to 15 years to accompany the soldiers.

"Who knows, but it might be a means to make them Englishmen, I mean Christians," replied Henry.[9] The death penalty for those who had not settled in Connaught by 1 May 1654 was in 1656 commuted to a sentence of deportation. Orders were also given to round up "wanderers" and "all children in hospitals and workhouses, all prisoners" for deportation.[10] Over subsequent years orders for the deportation of hundreds of people were commonplace. Altogether up to 100,000 people could have suffered this fate though many would have been sent to North America. In the West Indies, most deportation orders specify Barbados as the place of destination.

While Jamaica was mentioned as a destination, there is little evidence of Irish settlement there up to the end of the 17th century though black people with surnames such as Collins, O'Hare, McCormack, Kennedy, Walsh, McKeon, McDermott, Mackey and Burke have puzzled historians. These Black Irish of Jamaica, as they are called, are thought to have derived their Irish surnames from the practice of freed slaves taking their surnames from their former masters (who could have been settled on other Caribbean islands) rather than as indicating any major early Irish settlement.

Michael D. Higgins draws attention to the social composition of the Irish communities in the West Indies, made up of different waves of Irish emigration, some voluntary, some forced. The first wave included the younger sons of the Galway gentry who went there to make their fortune and who often owned the estates on which later waves of Irish worked, the peasants, the orphans, the political prisoners and those fleeing political persecution. He wonders whether many of the Irish on Montserrat made common cause with the large number of black slaves on the island, whose planned revolt as the gentry were celebrating St Patrick's Day in 1768 was betrayed but who finally did revolt and occupy the island in 1787. The story of the Irish in Montserrat is "a story in some ways of the colonized becoming colonizer," he writes.[11]

A number of Irish priests went to the West Indies in the 17th and 18th centuries, many of them to minister to these Irish. The Jesuit Fr John Stritch has already been mentioned. Ill-health forced him to return to Ireland in 1662 and he was replaced by a priest of the Cashel diocese, Fr John Grace. Other Jesuits who went out, including Fr John O'Daly from Kerry (1663-1738), Fr Roger Maguire (1707-?) and Fr Philip O'Reilly from Meath (1719-75) went to the French possessions of Martinique, Guadeloupe and French Guiana presumably because they had joined the French Jesuits. Only the Corkman, Fr James Galway (1655-1732) went to St Christopher. The Franciscan, Fr Gabriel Cullinan, from the west of Ireland, worked in Haiti from 1739 to 1753 and died in France in 1754 on his way home.

St Croix Mission

The most substantial Irish missionary endeavour in the region in the 18th century was on the Danish island of St Croix (today a US colony). After buying the island from France in 1733, the Danish king granted full freedom of religion thus attracting Catholics from some neighbouring British possessions who had to pay tithes to the Protestant clergy there despite their freedom to practice Catholicism. By 1758 there were 250 white Catholics on St Croix, most of them Irish, and in the same year two Irish Dominicans, Hyacinth Kennedy of Lorrha, Co Tipperary, and Dominic Allen, probably from Portumna, Co Galway, were sent to minister to them. Over the following decade eight Irish Dominicans worked on St Croix, three of whom died there. This mission is of particular interest because of the correspondence from some of the Dominicans there to Rome which has been preserved and published. This concerns mainly the vicissitudes of the priests, their bad health, their squabbles among themselves, their frustration at the lack of religious zeal among the local whites and their difficulties in applying the rules elaborated in Europe to the conditions of the West Indies.

Of the Irish on St Croix in 1760, we learn that there were "about twelve who have plantation estates, but in the town there are also many of our country, some merchants, traders, and captains of vessels who come here, and are about one hundred lads of our country overseers on plantations." These letters tell us nothing more specifically about the Irish (though we must infer that the complaints of religious indifference apply as much if not more to the local Irish) except for one fascinating reference in a report in Latin to Propaganda Fide (the forerunner of today's Vatican Congregation for the Propagation of the Faith) by Fr Charles O'Kelly, the mission's organiser in Rome and the person to whom all these letters were written. This mentions that many priests, both secular and regular, had been sought for this mission but especially Irish ones "whose language the other inhabitants use quite a bit." If this refers to the occasional use of the Irish language on the island of St Croix in the 18th century as the Irish Dominican historian, Fr Hugh Fenning, seems to think, then the island can rightly claim its place among the world's Gaeltachtaí!

While the priests complain a lot in their letters about financial problems and their expenses, one discloses his living conditions: "It's very hard living here. I have not been able to board myself as yet though I have a commodious house joining the church with two slaves." Another comments: "When I have money I dine at home. When I have none I look out where the largest smoke is." Neither does the lifestyle appear to have been too onerous, at least for some. One priest comments on a confrere just deceased: "He was, God give him rest, a good brother, but was no way fit for this part. He was of an easy deportment, a stranger to exercise, and kept the custom of sleeping every day after dinner three or four hours daily, a thing here unhealthy."

The religious indifference of the people comes in for a lot of mention. "I often grieve or fret," writes one. "To miss Mass or hear it is the same thing, or to break the fast or keep it. And to urge or with zeal speak you affront them. They are all judges and divines. May the God of mercy give me his grace. I often wished never to come here. And that inward tranquillity which I enjoyed in Europe I am stranger to here unless I shall neither hear or see." Another writes: "I would be much happier if my flock were as civilized as others. To my great sorrow they are not, for the greatest part of them are both obstinate and self-sufficient. No restraint can be put upon their pleasures and liberties. If a clergyman attempts it or even checks them, even in general, he will get more ill will from several of them than thanks." Yet another complains that "they are formed into a cabal and, presbyterian-like, if a clergyman don't do [sic] what any or all of them would have, they send him adrift."

The Friday fast caused considerable problems: "I would be glad to have your opinion upon our power of dispensation in fasts and holydays," writes Fr Thomas E. Devenish [also from Portumna] in April 1765. "As to the first you must know that in these islands we scarcely know at ten what we are to dine upon at twelve. On Sunday we have often plenty of exquisite fish and on Friday none, and in this case often neither roots nor eggs, so that often in the French and Spanish territories curates of scrupulous conscience transpose one day for the other. Now considering the uncertainty of our small islands, whether we can do so ourselves or whether we can allow the same indulgence to our parishioners? It is true few of them ask or desire said indulgence for they are not so exact, but if such be lawful, why should we not lessen the sins of the world?"

While few references are made to the wider society in which they live, the following mention in a letter from Fr Dominic Allen in April 1760 is revealing: "We were in vast apprehension last Christmas here from a design the negroes had of rising up against the white people, which had it not been providentially discovered before the time designed for the executing their plan [sic], it must have proved fatal to all those of our colour as we are scarce in the proportion of one to fifty. However, the Militia of the island took arms and several of the conspirators put alive [sic] into gibbets."[12] It seems clear that these priests could not have been accused of being infected with liberation theology!

Irish soldiers

Apart from these missionaries, few Irish played a role in Latin America in the 18th century. Of those who did, most were either in the Spanish or the British forces. These include the Irish Regiment in the Spanish army which served in Mexico from 1768 to 1771. Though only a small percentage of those who served in the regiment were of Irish birth or ancestry, all its companies were commanded by officers with Irish names – O'Hare, Barry, Fitzpatrick, Quinn, O'Brien, Healy, O'Leary and Treby, possibly Tracy. Of these some were Irish-born.

Another force containing some Irish was the British force commanded by an Irishman, Captain John McNamara, which attacked the Spanish settlement of Colonia del Sacramento upriver from Montevideo in present-day Uruguay in November 1762. While McNamara and most of the crew were killed in the battle, some waded ashore where they were captured and interned in Cordoba, some 800km inland from Buenos Aires, and in Mendoza at the foot of the Andes. When finally released many of these remained in Argentina; they or their descendents were to become involved in the Argentine army of José de San Martín which gathered in Mendoza in 1816 to invade and liberate Chile.

Ambrosio O'Higgins, Viceroy of Peru

The most remarkable Irishman to travel to Latin America in the 18th century, however, was Ambrosio O'Higgins. While overshadowed by his more famous son, Bernardo, this Sligo man born in Ballinary in 1721 rose to become viceroy of Peru, the most important Spanish official in South America. When young, he was employed as an errand boy by Lady Bective in Dangan Castle near Summerhill in Meath. An uncle sent him to Cadiz in Spain from where he travelled to Peru. He first ran a small toy shop in Lima and after studying engineering was involved in improving the Andean roads and building houses for travellers. Recognised by the colonial authorities, he was made administrator of the southern frontier of Chile. Here he made contact with the Mapuché people who maintained their independence until the 1880s. Accumulating titles such as Marquis of Osorno and Baron of Ballinar, he was appointed governor of Chile in 1787 and set about modernising the colonial administration. He abolished the *encomienda*, the practice which existed from the very first years of the Spanish conquest of giving grants of land and people to Spanish adventurers which became in practice a form of continuing slavery of the native peoples. In its place he instituted a practice known as the *inquilino* whereby the labourer was given a free plot of land and seed. In 1795 he was appointed viceroy of Peru in which office he died in 1801 at the age of 80.

Footnotes

1. Quoted in Oliver MacDonagh, *O'Connell: The Life of Daniel O'Connell 1775-1847*, London, Weidenfeld and Nicolson, 1991, p 170
2. Noel Dorr, in a speech to the General Assembly of the United Nations, 29 November 1982 (see Appendix I)
3. See Joyce Lorimer, ed., *English and Irish Settlements on the River Amazon 1550 to 1646*, Hakluyt Society and Cambridge University Press, 1989. The document of Bernard O'Brien quoted above is reproduced on pp 263-8.
4. Quoted in D. Murphy SJ, 'Deportation of the Irish to the West Indies in the Seventeenth Century' in *Irish Ecclesiastical Record*, 1893, p 745
5. Quoted in Aubrey Gwynn SJ, 'First Irish Priests in the New World' in *Studies*, 1932, p 220
6. Quoted in Aubrey Gwynn SJ, 'Early Irish Emigration to the West Indies (1612-1643)' in *Studies*, 1929, p 650
7. Interview with E.A.Markham in *The Irish Times*, 4 April 1991
8. Quoted in D Murphy SJ, op. cit., p 612
9. Ibid., p 744
10. Ibid., p 747
11. Michael D. Higgins, 'Montserrat: An Unfinished Story' in *The Emigrant Experience*, Galway Labour History Group, Galway, 1991, p 58
12. Quotes from 'The Mission to St Croix in the West Indies 1750-69' in *Archivium Hibernicum 1963*, edited by Hugh Fenning OP., pp 75-122

Chapter 8

The Irish in Latin America: 19th Century

"Bolívar remained an ideal for O'Connell all his life, neither was it a coincidence that he came to bear with pride the title invented originally for Bolívar – 'The Liberator'."

– Oliver MacDonagh, biographer of Daniel O'Connell[1]

The early 19th century saw a great increase in the involvement of Irish people in Latin America. This began even before the wars of independence as the British expedition which invaded Argentina in 1806 contained many Irish including both its army and its navy commanders (General Beresford and Admiral Popham). When they landed and captured Buenos Aires so many Irish troops deserted to the Argentine side that Beresford ordered them confined to barracks. Eleven months later, another British force landed which included the Connaught Rangers commanded by Colonel Duff. Presumably because of their compatriots' behaviour the year before, these troops were not given flints for their arms when they disembarked so that they could not fire them. This force was decisively defeated by a local people's militia and many of the Irish captured. Many, however, decided later to stay on and some played a role in the struggle for independence. This Argentine victory is regarded as presaging the independence struggle as it marked the first time the local elite got a sense of its own independent power.

Numerous Irish played a role in this struggle, the first in South America. Among these were people born in Argentina of Irish parents, such as Don Domingo French (1774-1825) both of whose parents were from Galway, and Colonel Ignacio Warnes (1772-1816) whose father was Irish. Both of these fought against the British expeditions of 1806-07. Their presence indicates the small numbers of Irish people who had emigrated to Argentina even before the end of the 18th century, some under

95

contract to work in beef salting, others as butchers or as hide-tanners. Another Irishman from that early period honoured in Argentina today is Dr Michael O'Gorman, born in Ennis, Co Clare in 1749. Following medical training in France, he moved to Spain where he was appointed head of medicine to the first viceroy of the River Plate region, Pedro de Ceballos. As the senior medical officer in Buenos Aires, he established the city's first medical institution, the Protomedicato, which in 1799 became the School of Medicine. He died in Buenos Aires in 1819.

William Brown and John Thomond O'Brien

The two most important Irishmen in Argentina's struggle for independence were also born in Ireland, William Brown and John Thomond O'Brien. Brown, founder of the Argentine navy and one of the country's foremost national heroes, was born in Foxford, Co Mayo, in June 1777 and when 9 years of age was taken by his father to settle in Pennsylvania. He began his naval life as a cabin boy in US merchant ships before being pressed into service by the British navy in 1796. By 1809 he was engaged in commerical trading with Argentina and got involved in its struggles when he arrived in Buenos Aires port during the revolution of 1810 to find it blockaded by Spanish ships. When his ship was commandeered by the Spanish, he organised an expedition which captured one of the blockading ships and brought it in triumph into port. Offered the command of a small fleet by the Argentine authorities, he broke the Spanish blockade of Montevideo in March 1814 allowing the patriot army capture it and effectively ended the Spanish threat to the newly independent state.

He took part in a more daring exploit in 1816 when he led a fleet which for three weeks blockaded the Peruvian port of Callao for three weeks, the heart of Spanish rule in South America, and then went on to capture the fort of Punta de las Piedras at the mouth of Guayaquil Bay in southern Ecuador, another important Spanish port. Before finding his way back to Buenos Aires, he was captured by both the Spanish (in Ecuador) and then by the British (in Barbados) and had to fight his case in a British court. On return, he faced a government investigation into his exploits and was retired from active service in 1819. He was, however, recalled to service upon the outbreak of war with Brazil (1825-28) during which he gained a number of major victories. On his death in 1857, he was given a public funeral and buried with full honours.

Less-well known is John Thomond O'Brien. Born in Co Wicklow in 1796, he arrived in Argentina in 1814 and saw his first action at the siege of Montevideo in that year. He then joined the army of the Andes in Mendoza and was quickly recognised by San Martín, the liberator of Argentina and Chile, who appointed him his personal aide-de-camp. In this capacity, he took part in all the major actions of the independence struggle in Chile and Peru and was present in a position of honour at the declaration of independence in Lima in July 1826. Following the wars of independence, he took a particular interest in Irish affairs and toured Ireland in 1827 seeking to interest Irish people in emigrating to Argentina though he did not meet with great immediate success. In 1828 he gathered together in Buenos Aires a group of distinguished Irish people, including Admiral Brown, to decide how best they could help the struggle for Catholic Emancipation in Ireland. He died in Lisbon in 1861 as he was returning to Argentina and his remains were repatriated there in 1935.

Bernardo O'Higgins, Liberator of Chile

The Chilean struggle for independence is intimately connected with the name of another Irishman, Bernardo O'Higgins. The "illegitimate" son of Ambrosio O'Higgins, Bernardo was born in Talca in southern Chile in 1778. Though he saw little of his father, the latter did provide for his education and Bernardo was sent to school in England. He returned to Chile in 1802 to claim the estate left to him by his father and was an early supporter of moves for independence. He was elected to the patriot congress in 1810 and championed liberal reforms. He commanded patriot forces against the Spanish in 1813 and 1814, including the patriot defeat by the Spanish at Rancagua in October 1814. He then fled to Argentina where he joined up with San Martín's invasion force and participated in the final defeat of Spanish rule in the battle of Chacabuco in February 1817. He was the first Supreme Director of Chile and put down a royalist revolt at the battle of Maipú in April 1818. It was he who formally declared

Chilean independence in the same year.

Yet his many liberal reforms including the abolition of titles of nobility, the expulsion of the royalist bishop of Santiago and the restriction of religious processions and of the veneration of images alienated entrenched interests. Many liberals were also alienated by what they saw as his autocratic rule and in 1823 he had to flee to Peru where he saw military service under Bolívar. He died in exile in 1842 but is regarded in Chile as the father of the country's independence and the main avenue through the centre of Santiago is named after him.

In other parts of Latin America, Irish troops also played a role in the struggles for independence though in Mexico the potential Irish involvement was aborted before it even began. In 1808, the British raised an army in Ireland to establish a base in Venezuela in order to intervene in Mexico. However, the expedition never got under way as Napoleon invaded Spain and the Irish army was dispatched there instead.

Bolívar's Irish Legionaries

It was with Bolívar in Venezuela and Colombia that most Irish saw action in the wars of independence. From as early as 1815, Bolívar had an Irish aide-de-camp, Charles Chamberlain, who had resigned from a West Indian regiment to join him but was killed in action in 1817. As a result of an appeal by Bolívar for British volunteers, recruitment began in Ireland and Britain in 1817. Over the next two and a half years 53 ships left Irish and British ports carrying some 6,500 men for service in South America until pressure by the Spanish Ambassador in London forced the British authorities to put an end to it in late 1819. Of those who left, some 5,300 landed in Colombia or Venezuela, most of them Irish. Many of these were former soldiers in the British army who were being demobilised as the Napoleonic wars had come to an end.

In November 1817, the first group of 800 officers and men set out but were depleted through mutinies and shipwrecks and only 240 arrived in South America. Known as the 1st Venezuelan Rifles, these served right through the war of independence and were only disbanded in 1830. Commanding them from 1819 to 1825 was Arthur Sandes of Glenfield, Co Kerry, who had retired from the British army in 1815 and who ended his days as governor of the province of Cuenca in Ecuador and was a renowned educational innovator. Another officer, James English from Churchtown, Dublin, returned to Ireland to continue recruiting in the summer of 1818. He returned the following year with a mixed group of Irish, English and Hanoverians.

Meanwhile John Devereux, thought by some to be a veteran of the 1798 rising in New Ross, had arrived in Cartagena, Colombia, from the United States in 1815 where he boasted of being a general in the Irish army. Devereux interested Bolívar who accepted his offer to raise an Irish Legion of 5,000 men. He set sail for Ireland in 1818 and arrived in Dublin in 1819 where he lodged in Morrison's Hotel in Dawson Street, afterwards to be the Dublin headquarters of Parnell. Here he displayed the flag of the Legion, a gold harp on a green ground encircled by the stars of Colombia. He won early support from Daniel O'Connell whose son Morgan and a near relative from Ennis, Maurice, enlisted. The first contingent landed in Margarita between September and December 1819 and the rest arrived in Angostura (today's Ciudad Bolívar) in April and May 1820. From the beginning, however, the expedition was plagued with problems as they were given little food and no pay. They suffered a number of mutinies, particularly after an attack on the Legion at Rio Hacha soon after they landed. This left huge casualties and afterwards most of the Irish were evacuated to Jamaica for shipment home. Bolívar said he was "pleased to be rid of these vile mercenaries who would do no killing until they had been paid for it."[2]

After this, however, the remnants of the various groups of Irish and British who had arrived were reorganised, some serving in the 1st Rifles and others in what had by now become an Anglo-Irish Legion. Other Irish officers served with other units. Hundreds of Irish took part on the celebrated march across the Andes in 1819 and in the decisive battles of Boyacá, Colombia, and Carabobo, Venezuela. In the latter battle, the Irish Legion was said to number 350 and suffered 11 officers and 95 men killed and 50 wounded. All the survivors were awarded the Order of the Liberator and the legion was renamed the Carabobo Battalion, a battalion which still exists in the Venezuelan army.

Among the Irish who distinguished themselves were Dr Thomas Foley of Kilkenny who was chief medical officer on the Andes march and Major Richard Murphy of Sligo, the Legion's chief surgeon. William O'Connor, who came to be known as Francis Burdett O'Connor after his father's friend Sir Francis Burdett, came from Connorsville, Co Cork. After action under Bolívar, he served as chief of staff to Antonio José de Sucre (later first president of Bolivia) at the battle of Ayacucho, Peru, in

December 1824, the last major engagement of the South American independence struggle. He later served as minister of war in Bolivia and wrote his memoirs called *American Independence*. Captain Charles Minchin of Tipperary who was wounded at Carabobo, later rose to become minister of war in Venezuela.

Throughout this period Bolívar had a succession of Irish aides-de-camp. Following Charles Chamberlain's death, James Rooke, born in Dublin the "illegitimate" son of a British officer who was ADC to Lord Townsend, joined Bolívar as ADC in 1817. William Ferguson, ADC from 1824-28, was killed defending the Liberator during an assassination attempt in Bogotá and Belford Hinton Wilson, ADC from 1824, was with Bolívar when he died in 1830. Undoubtedly the greatest, however, was Daniel Florence O'Leary, ADC from 1819 to 1828.

Daniel Florence O'Leary

O'Leary was born in Cork city around 1800, the son of a well-to-do butter merchant in Cook Street, Jeremiah O'Leary. At a young age he enlisted in the 1st Division of the Red Hussars of Venezuela, a company raised in Britain and Ireland, and left Portsmouth in December 1817. After his arrival in Venezuela he requested transfer to a local unit due to his distaste for the lack of discipline among the Red Hussars. He soon impressed his commander and was appointed his aide-de-camp. Though he sustained a serious wound in battle following the Andes march in 1819, he participated in the triumphal procession through Bogotá and was decorated with the Order of the Liberator. In April 1820 he was appointed aide-de-camp to Bolívar who entrusted him with negotiating a truce with the Spanish commander, General Morillo. Over the following years, Bolívar put him in charge of several important military and diplomatic missions and by 1825 he had been promoted to the rank of colonel.

The greatest sign of the trust in which Bolívar held him, however, was the mission he sent him on in June 1826 from Peru. For long the Liberator's desire was the political unity of South America and he sent O'Leary to Caracas and Bogotá to try to establish a federal state uniting Gran Colombia (a state incorporating Venezuela, Colombia and Ecuador which lasted until 1830) with Peru and Bolivia. O'Leary's failure on this sensitive mission did not lessen his importance; in 1829 he commanded troops in the short-lived war against Peru and was made a general. The same year he was appointed Colombian minister to Washington, a post he never took up due to the political crisis of the Gran Colombian state. By 1833 he had settled in Caracas after an unsuccessful attempt to set up in business in Jamaica.

O'Leary spent from 1834 to 1839 on a diplomatic mission to London, Paris and Madrid seeking recognition of the new state of Venezuela. During this mission he met Daniel O'Connell in London and, in August 1834, visited Cork and Killarney. On his return to South America he held a number of British diplomatic appointments, including chargé d'affaires in Bogotá. When on a visit in 1852 to his two sons who were in school in England, he visited Dublin and donated a collection of South American minerals, plants and birds to Queen's College, Cork, now UCC. He died in 1854 in Bogotá and in 1882 his remains were interred in the National Pantheon in Caracas near those of Bolívar. His three-volume *Narración* remains to the present day one of the most popular first-hand accounts of the independence struggles in the northern countries of South America. One of the principal squares in the Venezuelan capital, Caracas, is the Plaza O'Leary. The Venezuelan government has also placed a plaque on his birthplace in Cork.

Founding South America's navies

A major contribution of Irishmen to some of the newly independent states was in naval affairs. Less well-known than Admiral William Brown, the founder of the Argentine navy, are Thomas Charles Wright of Drogheda who founded the Ecuadorean navy and Peter Campbell of Tipperary who founded the Uruguayan navy. Born in Queensborough in 1799, Wright had fought in the British navy against Napoleon and in the Anglo-American war of 1812. Hearing of Bolívar's campaigns, he offered his services and after some military service was asked by Bolívar to improvise a naval force to patrol the Pacific coast. In a decisive encounter off Callao, Spain's main naval base, Wright's skill was highly praised. According to Dr John de Courcy Ireland, Wright "by preventing the arrival of supplies or reinforcements by sea for the Spaniards, was in no small way the architect of the final overthrow of Spanish power in South America."[3] He later commanded the *Chimborazo* which took Bolívar down the Pacific coast as far as Chile. Following independence, he settled in the Ecuadorean port of Guayaquil and fought with O'Leary in the war against Peru. When Ecuador achieved its independence in 1830, he was asked to organise the new state's navy. A committed liberal, he fled into exile in Chile in 1845 for 15 years when a liberal regime was overthrown in Ecuador. He died back in his adopted country in 1868.

Campbell arrived in South America as a soldier in the 1806 British force invading Buenos Aires. After being imprisoned by the Argentines, he joined forces with the liberator of Uruguay, José Artigas, for whom he organised a naval force in 1814. Following the defeat of Artigas in 1819, Campbell was exiled to Paraguay where he took up his old trade as a tanner. He died in Paraguay in 1832 but his remains were later repatriated to Uruguay.

In many ways an Irishman can also be said to have founded the Chilean navy since Bernardo O'Higgins recruited a Captain George O'Brien to establish it. O'Brien, however, died in action for his new country commanding the *Lautaro* in an action which led to the capture of a number of Spanish warships. His memory lives on in the Chilean navy which still names ships after him. Two other Chileans of Irish descent played a greater role in the Chilean navy later in the 19th century. Charles Condell, who according to Dr de Courcy Ireland was a distant relative of the last principal of Dublin's Hibernian Marine School, was born in Chile in 1844. Joining the navy in 1858, he saw action in the Chilean-Spanish war of 1865-66 after which he was sent to Callao to repatriate the remains of Bernardo O'Higgins. Condell saw action in the War of the Pacific (1879-83) and for a time commanded the captured *Huascar*, one of the prized possessions of the Peruvian navy. He was a rear-admiral at the time of his death in 1887.

Patricio Lynch, born in 1824 to a wealthy Irish merchant in Chile, is regarded as the country's foremost naval hero. He spent seven years in the British navy as part of his training during which he took part in the Opium War. During the War of the Pacific he was first put in charge of transports and is said to have applied revolutionary technical concepts not fully developed until the Second World War. He led the Chilean landing in southern Peru and was commander of the final assault on Lima in January 1880. After its capture, he was appointed military governor of the city. His atrocities in putting down Peruvian resistance were denounced by another distinguished Irish-Chilean, the liberal politician and historian Benjamín Vicuña Mackenna (1831-86). Lynch was appointed Chilean ambassador to Spain in 1884, his country's most important diplomatic post, and died on board a British liner on his way home to Chile.

Irish seamen serving in the Portuguese navy moved to Brazil when the Portuguese royal family fled there in 1808. Among them were Diago Nicolau Keating who died as a rear-admiral in Brazil in 1817 and Diago O'Grady who was appointed aide-de-camp to the governor of São Paulo in 1811. Keating's son, Diago Keating, joined the navy in Brazil in 1815 and is regarded as one of the founders of the Brazilian navy. Jorge Cowan, another Irish officer, stayed behind in Brazil when the king returned to Portugal and served in the flagship of the new Brazilian navy, the *Dom Pedro I*.

Irish expedition to Brazil

An ill-fated Irish expedition to Brazil took place in 1826 when a Colonel Cotter, an Irish officer serving in the Brazilian army, was sent to Ireland to recruit a regiment for service against Argentina. He went to Co. Cork where he promised the local people that if they enlisted they would be given a grant of land after five years' service. He left for Rio de Janeiro with 2,400 men, women and children who, when they arrived, were completely neglected. The local blacks taunted them by calling them the *escravos brancos*, white slaves. When a German regiment, which had been similarly recruited, mutinied, the Irish joined them and for a while there was open warfare on the streets of Rio. The Minister of War, Barbozo, ordered: "Destroy every man...exterminate the whole of the strangers."[4] While most were finally sent home, some did stay and were sent to form a colony in Bahia. The town of São Patricio in the interior state of Goias with its statue of St Patrick may also have been established by some of those who remained from this expedition.

San Patricio battalion

A more celebrated military exploit involving Irish troops was that of the San Patricio battalion made up of deserters from the US army during the Mexican-American war of 1846-48. Led by John O'Reilly, a deserter from the British army in Canada, some hundreds of Irish crossed over to the Mexican side encouraged, it is said, by Mexican offers of good land and reminders that the Mexicans were fellow Catholics. From a study of transcripts of their courts martial, however, the US historian Richard Blaine McCormack concluded that it was not religion or material gain which lured them over but drink! Yet such transcripts are hardly the most reliable sources for their true motives as they would have been trying to convince their judges that their desertion was a less serious crime than it might appear. Fighting under a green banner emblazoned with an Irish harp and shamrock, the Irish won special decorations for their courage in the battle of Buena Vista but suffered heavy casualties in the fierce battle of Churubusco when 85 out of 200 were taken prisoner by the US. Of these 72 were court martialled and 50 hanged. During the final battle for Mexico City, these were taken to where they could see the fortress of Chapultepec in the centre of the city. They were kept until they could see the US flag run up over the fortress and then they were hanged. Five were pardoned and 15 had their death sentences commuted; these were given 50 lashes and had the letter D for deserter branded on their cheeks.

The bravery of the San Patricio battalion is widely known among Mexicans today and every 12 September a ceremony in their honour takes place in the San Jacinto Plaza in Mexico City where a plaque in their honour stands. As the Mexican Ambassador to Ireland, Mr Bernardo Sepúlveda, said: "The fact that St Patrick's battalion came with US troops and decided to change sides because they were convinced it was an unjust war against Mexico is something that appeals to the Mexican imagination."[5]

Irish emigration to Argentina

Argentina was the only Latin American country which saw sizable Irish immigration during the last century and a distinctive Irish-Argentine community exists today which continues to cultivate its Irish identity. Apart from those Irish who arrived with British expeditions and settled in Argentina as has already been mentioned, a number of other Irish people emigrated in the early years of the 19th century who were to play a key role in the subsequent wave of emigration. Among these were John Dillon who emigrated with his family in 1807 and made a fortune through smuggling, Thomas Armstrong from Garrycastle near Athlone who emigrated around 1817 and founded a bank, the Stock Exchange and other organisations to develop the agricultural and mining industries and Peter Sheridan from Cavan who emigrated in 1817 and set up a prominent meat processing business in the Argentine capital. In the same period a certain number of Irish who had emigrated to North America were attracted to Argentina by the enthusiastic reports written for the US Congress by Theodoric Bland in 1818. These were known as the "Yankee Irish." By 1824 therefore there was a large enough Irish community in Buenos Aires to have its own chaplain, the Irish Dominican Fr Edmund Burke.

It was, however, the visit to Ireland of General John Thomond O'Brien in 1827 which laid the foundation for the later emigration. With him he brought back William Mooney and his son-in-law Patrick Rookey from Streamstown in Co Westmeath. Around the same time, the Liverpool-based Dickson and Montgomery Bank sent Patrick Browne from Wexford to run their business in Argentina. These three saw the potential for developing the meat and wool industries but realised they would need labour to do it and sent back to their places of origin inviting people to emigrate to Argentina. From the early 1830s therefore we see an increase in the number of Irish registered as entering the port of Buenos Aires from a total of 34 in the five years 1826-1830 to 167 in the following five years, 1831-35.

Most of these, the younger sons of larger tenant farmers with education and management skills, were put in charge of large flocks of sheep on the pampas or huge, virtually empty, prairie lands. A system known as "halves" was used whereby the owner would give charge of some 2,000 to 3,000 sheep to the shepherd who was expected to cover all expenses for maintaining them over an agreed number of seasons, including the rent of land. At the end of the agreed period, the owner and the shepherd would divide on a 50/50 basis the flock which should have grown to 10,000 or 12,000 sheep. In this way many of the new immigrants soon established themselves comfortably as permanent settlers with their own land. Needing labourers to work the land for them, they too sought them from their home areas in Ireland. This second group, however, were mostly the sons of landless farm labourers without the means to set up on their own. Since Irish emigration to Argentina was almost entirely in response to encouragement from previous emigrants who were established there, it came from two clearly defined areas, south-east of a line from Wexford town to Kilmore Quay in Wexford and from a quadrangle on the Longford/Westmeath border stretching roughly from Athlone to Edgeworthstown to Mullingar to Kilbeggan. Virtually the whole population surrounding the town of Ballymore, which stands roughly at the centre of this quadrangle, emigrated to Buenos Aires in the 1860s (see map p.106).

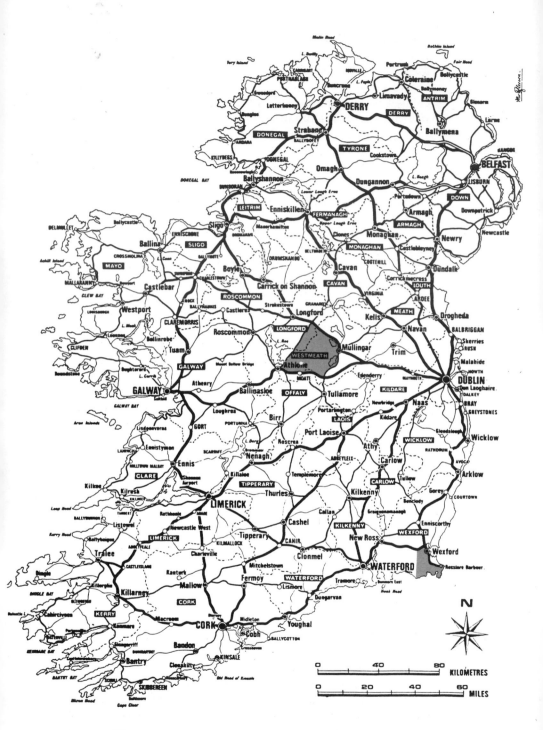

Main areas of Irish emigration to Argentina

Ireland and Latin America

As the Irish community grew, so did the demand for priests. A Dublin diocesan priest, Fr Patrick Moran, died in 1830, 14 months after his arrival. It is interesting to note that following his death the president of the Irish Catholic Society in Buenos Aires, Dr John Oughan, asked the Archbishop of Buenos Aires to request a replacement from his opposite number in Dublin. This indicates the level of organisation of the Irish community at this early stage and its social position in the Argentine capital. The 31-year-old Fr Patrick O'Gorman arrived in 1831 in answer to that request but as the Irish community grew in size and extended over a wider territory, the need grew for more priests to be sent from Ireland.

As a result Fr Anthony Fahy, a 39-year-old Dominican from Loughrea, Co Galway, who had already spent some time in the United States, arrived in January 1844. Fahy estimated his flock at this time to be about 4,000, three-quarters of whom were living in the countryside. A gifted administrator, he organised what became virtually a separate church and welfare system for the Irish, elements of which have lasted down to the present day. He raised funds for the education of priests for Argentina in Clonliffe College, Dublin. As these arrived they were sent ever further from the capital to minister to the Irish. To provide medical care, Fr Fahy set up a separate hospital for the Irish in 1848 and in 1855 a group of Irish Mercy nuns arrived who took charge of the hospital and set up a college to educate the children of the Irish. They were soon to be followed by the Passionist and Pallottine Fathers who established colleges and parish churches for the Irish. Meanwhile, Fr Fahy was encouraging further Irish emigration, making special efforts to encourage Irish women to emigrate to Argentina in order to ensure the survival of the Irish community. When they landed, these women were lodged with Irish landladies who either found them suitable employment or helped introduce them to Irish men visiting the capital from the pampas. Again Fr Fahy's hand was behind these arrangements.

During all this time, events in Ireland were closely followed by the Irish community. Efforts to organise support for Daniel O'Connell and Catholic Empancipation in the 1820s have already been mentioned and as repeal became the dominant issue in Irish politics a Repeal Club was established in Buenos Aires in the early 1840s. News of the Great Famine led to the establishment of an Irish Relief Fund and in early 1847 £421-1s-10d was sent to the Archbishop of Dublin for famine relief, a considerable sum for those times and a witness to the prosperity of the Irish community. A year later, another fund was established to raise money to erect a monument to Daniel O'Connell in Dublin.

In financial matters, too, Fr Fahy played a key role among the Irish. With so many living long distances from the capital, he acted as the banker to the Irish community, lodging their money and keeping their accounts. In this he was helped by his close, life-long friend, Thomas Armstrong, a well-established Protestant in the business world of Buenos Aires. Fr Fahy was also relied upon by the Irish for decisions about agricultural investments or about opportunities opening up in areas of the country just being colonised. His banking contacts also served him well in gaining the credit to build the extensive network of schools, hospitals, orphanages and parish churches for the Irish.

Another problem to which Fr Fahy was asked to turn his attention was the spiritual care of the Catholics of the Malvinas (or Falkland) Islands, some of them Irish. The islands had been occupied by the British in 1833 and so had left Argentine jurisdiction. After his help had been requested, Fr Fahy sent an Irish priest, Fr Lawrence Kirwan, to the islands in 1857 and he was succeeded by Irish diocesan priests until in 1886 the islands were put under the care of the Argentine Salesians, who sent Irish Argentine priests who spoke English to work there.

Irish immigration to Argentina reached its peak in the immediate post-Famine years; in 1849, 712 Irish arrived in Buenos Aires port, the largest figure for any one year. A long letter from Fr Fahy published in the *Dublin Review* in 1848 defending the Argentine dictator Juan Manuel de Rosas who, he said, had extended his protection "in a generous form to the Catholic Irish"[6] is credited to some extent with this growth. The immediate post-Famine conditions were, of course, another reason though the areas from which the Irish emigrated to Argentina were not particularly badly hit by the Great Famine.

All in all, some 30,000 Irish are estimated to have emigrated to Argentina in the last century, most of them from the 1840s to the 1860s. By then the Irish community had established itself and with the growing mechanisation of farming and a switch from sheep farming to tillage, the need for further labour from Ireland was reduced. Furthermore the Argentine economy was in recession while the United States presented more attractive opportunities as it recovered from the civil war. Yet one more attempt to encourage Irish emigration took place in 1888 when the government of President Juarez Celman authorised 50,000 free passages from Europe. Two Irishmen opened information centres in Dublin and in Cork despite opposition from leaders of the Irish-Argentine community which considered the expedition hazardous and from some Irish bishops. In 1889 the *City of Dresden* arrived in Buenos Aires with 1,800 men, women and children, 1,100 of whom were Irish. They quickly ended up homeless and destitute, however, as the government made no provision for them and Irish Argentines had to rally around to help them.

By the time Fr Fahy died in 1871, the community was well established. His social stature is testified to by the fact that President Mitre named him a canon of Buenos Aires cathedral in 1864, an honour no other foreigner has received. Meanwhile the Irish community, by now spread over a wide area, continued to develop. In 1875, *The Southern Cross* newspaper was founded which to this day serves as an indispensible source of information on the extensive activities of the Irish-Argentine community. It is, according to its editor, Fr Fred Richards, the oldest Irish newspaper outside Ireland.

Political events in Ireland continued to have their echo in Argentina. In 1867 a Fenian Prisoners' Fund was established in Buenos Aires while in 1880 in the province of Salto a Land League was set up, modelled on the League in Ireland. In 1899, a branch of Conradh na Gaeilge was founded in the Argentine capital while the 1916 Rising and its aftermath led to the growth of republican clubs named after republican heroes such as Pearse, Ashe, Casement and McSweeney. These organised conferences and held demonstrations to promote the cause of Irish independence. The Irish tricolour was publicly displayed for the first time in the Argentine capital at a march to the city centre Plaza de Mayo in 1920 following the death on hunger strike of the Lord Mayor of Cork, Terence McSweeney.

The Irish community has maintained its cohesion through the education given by priests, nuns and brothers, some from Ireland such as the Christian Brothers who staff the prestigious Newman College in the Argentine capital. Until recently this was given in English and among the Irish community one still meets people with a distinctive Westmeath accent who have never travelled outside Argentina. Various sporting and cultural organisations keep the adult community together though in recent decades the community's cohesion has weakened and intermarriage with non-Irish Argentines is now common.

Regarded as prosperous and influential, Irish Argentines have played key roles in Argentine life. An early distinguished Irish-Argentine, Dalmacio Vélez Sársfield (1800-75), has given a distinctively Irish name to streets in towns and cities throughout the country. Thought to be a direct descendent of a brother of

Patrick Sarsfield, he was the author of Argentina's code of civil law. General Edelmiro J. Farrell, was President of the country from March 1944 until May 1945 while another Irish-Argentine, Brigadier Eduardo F. McLoughlin, was Minister for External Affairs from June 1972 until May 1973. Various estimates are given for the strength of the Irish Argentine community but it is thought it could number anything up to 300,000.

James J. O'Kelly and the Mambí Land

Various other Irish surface elsewhere in Latin America in the last century. Probably the most remarkable was the Irish Fenian and later Parnellite MP, James J. O'Kelly, who is honoured in Cuba as the author of a book which brought that country's independence struggle to world attention. Both O'Kelly's date and place of birth are disputed, some putting it in Galway in 1840 and others in Dublin in 1845. Following studies in Dublin, O'Kelly had moved to London in 1862 to study sculpture under his uncle, Michael Lawlor. He soon became involved with the Fenians and in 1863 fled to France for safety where he joined the Foreign Legion and saw service in Algeria. He was then sent to Mexico as part of the French occupying force which sought to impose the Austrian Archduke Ferdinand Maximilian as emperor. Wounded in battle, O'Kelly was captured by the Mexican forces in June 1866. A letter from John Devoy telling him that the Fenian rising was fixed for the following March encouraged his escape and return to England. Seeing the lack of preparations for the rising, O'Kelly advised against it but remained active in the movement after its failure. In the Franco-Prussian war of 1870, he joined an Irish Catholic ambulance corps which served on the French side but following the fall of Napoleon III, O'Kelly left for the United States.

An active member of Clan na nGael in the United States, O'Kelly joined the staff of the *New York Herald*, a newspaper celebrated for its direct reporting of key world events. Among his assignments for the *Herald* was hunting buffalo with Buffalo Bill and accompanying Emperor Pedro II on his journey from Brazil for a state visit to the United States. O'Kelly was credited with saving the life of the empress in Rio de Janeiro bay and with gaining the confidence of the emperor so that only the *Herald* carried an interview with him.

O'Kelly was already a member of the board of directors of the

Herald when he was asked to go to Cuba in late 1872 to report on the war of independence there. Despite attempts by the Spanish colonial authorities to stop him, he managed to get into the area occupied by the Cuban insurgents and spent six weeks there in early 1873. The Cuban leader, Carlos Manuel de Céspedes, one of the country's foremost heroes today, was obviously impressed by the Irish journalist as he mentioned him in letters to his wife. On his return to the Spanish-held town of Manzanillo on 31 March, O'Kelly was immediately arrested and put in prison. His presence there, and fears that the Spanish would shoot him, led to a major controversy in the Cuban and US press and appeals on his behalf were made to the US President and Secretary of State. His life seems to have been saved by a republican coup in Spain and on 30 May he was put on board a ship for Spain. Though imprisoned in Madrid, the republican authorities were sympathetic to his plight and released him before a coup by royalists took place. O'Kelly immediately fled to Gibraltar and found his way back to the United States.

His lengthy articles on Cuba had already been published in the *Herald* and in 1874 these were published in book form under the title *The Mambi-Land, or Adventures of A Herald Correspondent in Cuba*. The Mambí in the title was a word, of African origin, used in Cuba to denote a rebel or a bandit but to which the insurgents gave a positive meaning and applied to themselves. The articles were immediately translated into Spanish and published in newspapers sympathetic to the Cuban independence cause and in 1876 the first Spanish translation of the book was published. Its success is testified to by the fact that three further Spanish translations were made in 1887 and 1888 and even in the 1930s it was being translated afresh. To mark the centenary of the Ten Years' War (1868-78), the precursor of Cuban independence in 1898, a new edition was published in Havana with a lengthy introduction on O'Kelly himself.

O'Kelly later returned to Ireland, was elected MP for Roscommon and became a trusted confidant of Parnell. He ended his life semi-paralysed in a wheelchair but continued his parliamentary career until he died in London on 22 December 1916.

Other notable Irish

Among other notable Irish of the last century who are remembered in Latin America is William Albert Charles Ryan, born in Canada of Irish parents, who opted to fight for the independence of Cuba rather than join the Fenians though he had attended a number of Fenian meetings around Buffalo. The time was not ripe for the Irish struggle, he decided, until Ireland had resolved its religious differences. When visiting Washington on business in 1868 he met General Goicouria from Cuba and enlisted. He saw action on the island in 1870 and was sent to New York to raise a force. Captured by the Spanish on his way back, he was executed in Santiago de Cuba on 4 November 1873. Jeremiah O'Donovan Rossa spoke at a meeting in New York to protest at his execution.

William Russell Grace, born in Riverstown, Co Cork, in 1832 ran away to New York at the age of 14. Four years later he moved to Peru where he joined the shipping firm of Bryce & Co as a clerk, becoming a partner two years later. By 1854, the name was changed to Bryce, Grace & Co and grew to control most of the shipping on the Peruvian and Chilean coasts. In time the company also moved into the sugar exporting business and into textile manufacturing. In 1865, William R. Grace left the firm under the management of his brother and moved to New York where he set up the shipping firm of W.R. Grace & Co. This grew to become a major multinational company, controlling a substantial portion of the US trade with South America. The name Grace is therefore intimately associated in Peru and in Chile with the inroads of foreign capital and the new forms of economic dependence and exploitation of the labour force associated with this phase of transnational capitalism. Entering politics late in life, he was elected mayor of New York in 1880 and 1884. In 1892 he established the first direct steamship service between New York and Peru. He died in New York in 1904.

Undoubtedly the most colourful Irish person to enter Latin American history in the 19th century, however, was Elisa Alicia Lynch. Born in Ireland in 1835, she married a French army doctor at the age of fifteen but three years later deserted him. Following various amorous escapades in Paris, in 1853 she met Francisco Solano López, the son of the dictator of Paraguay who was then visiting the French capital. She returned with him to Asunción where they lived openly together and she bore him five children. In 1862 on the death of his father, López became president and his mistress the de facto first lady. She played an active role in the War of the Triple Alliance (1865-70) alongside her lover, was present when he was killed in 1870 and buried him together with their first-born son. Though she had amassed great wealth, she lost it when deported at the end of the war. She lived for a time in Paris and died in Jerusalem in 1886, penniless and largely forgotten.

Footnotes

1. Oliver MacDonagh, *O'Connell: The Life of Daniel O'Connell 1775-1847*, London, Weidenfeld and Nicholson, 1991, p 171
2. Quoted in W.J. Williams, 'Bolívar and his Irish Legionaries', in *Studies*, 1929, p 627
3. John de Courcy Ireland, *Ireland and the Irish in Maritime History*, Dublin, Glendale Press, 1986, p 230
4. Frederic von Allendorfer, 'An Irish Regiment in Brazil 1826-8', in *The Irish Sword*, 1957, p 30
5. Interview given to the author, April 1991
6. Quoted in 'Irlandeses en la epoca rosista' in *The Southern Cross*, centenary number, 1975, p 26 (translated by PK)

Chapter 9

Distant Relations: The Irish State and Latin America

"I believe our stand on issues of concern to the Latin American countries, including in the context of the dialogues with the Central American countries and the Rio Group, has been positive and constructive. We have consistently taken a position in support of peace, democracy, political pluralism and respect for human rights and have given political support to moves by the countries of the region to achieve these objectives."

– Gerard Collins TD, Irish Foreign Minister, 1989-92[1]

For most of the period since independence, relations at an official level between the Irish state and Latin American and Caribbean countries have been minimal. Of the thirty-one independent states in the region, Argentina is the only one where Ireland has a resident diplomatic mission while up until 1991 the Argentine embassy was the only Latin American mission in Dublin. Apart from that Ireland has diplomatic relations with only Brazil, Mexico and Venezuela. In mid-1991, a Mexican embassy was opened in Dublin though it was immediately being staffed only to chargé d'affaires level.

Missions of the first Dáil

Yet the first diplomatic initiatives of Dáil Éireann showed much more interest in Latin America. The first ever mission of the Irish diplomatic service, announced by Arthur Griffith in the Dáil on 17 June 1919, was the appointment of Eamonn Bulfin as representative to Argentina and the following day the Dáil authorised a payment of £100 to establish a consulate in Buenos Aires. While Griffith said other missions were being planned, it was June 1920 before the Dáil passed a motion authorising missions to Russia, France, Spain, Italy, Austria, Germany, Denmark, Switzerland and a number of US cities. On 17 August 1921, the Dáil heard the first comprehensive report on his newly-established Department from Count George Plunkett, Minister for Foreign Affairs. The Republic then had eight foreign representatives, two of them in Latin America. These were Bulfin in Argentina and Frank W. Egan in Chile. Count Plunkett announced that the "Address to the Representatives of Foreign Nations" adopted by the Dáil in January was being forwarded to representatives of the countries of Europe, Japan, China and the Philippines, the British colonies "and all the countries on the American continent." Count Plunkett reported that Eamonn Bulfin was planning to publish an "Irish Bulletin" in Buenos Aires and that "the President of the Argentine is favourably disposed towards the Irish Republican cause." Bulfin's opinion, according to Count Plunkett, was that "if the United States government recognised the Irish Republic he feels sure that the Argentine government would do likewise." The Minister also reported the plans of "our honorary representative in Santiago" to establish an Irish association, the "Irish Colony of Chile". Mr Egan thought the President of Chile was "in sympathy with the Irish cause," according to Count Plunkett, and he quoted Egan as saying that "recognition (of the Irish Republic) by Chile would inevitably bring recognition by the Argentine and possibly Brazil as well, in addition to acting as the incentive to the United States to take the step over which they appear to be hesitating."[2]

A more substantial diplomatic mission was, however, announced by Count Plunkett to the Dáil during his report. This was the sending of Lawrence Ginnell "as a special envoy on a mission to the Argentine and the other South American republics."[3] Ginnell, who was treasurer of Sinn Féin, was a former MP for Westmeath from 1906 to 1918 who joined Sinn Féin after the 1916 Rising and was TD for Westmeath in the First Dáil. He was Director of Publicity from April 1919 to August 1921 and was imprisoned for a period. He had arrived in Buenos Aires on 25 July 1921, and stayed in Argentina until April 1922 during which time he had an official meeting with the Argentine foreign minister, Dr Honorio Pueyrredon. Political divisions over the Treaty cut short his South American mission and he was summoned home to be asked by de Valera to be the sole anti-Treatyite to enter the Second Dáil in August 1922 in order to challenge its legitimacy. This led to his forced removal.

His own account of his mission published in the December 1922 issue of the *Catholic Bulletin* makes interesting reading:

"In Argentina the British Minister at first sought to have me expelled. Failing in that, he was forced by a poster I issued giving an official statement of British policy in Ireland to make a public speech in defence of his country against me. This played into my hands by directing universal attention to my poster, which was mentioned in all newspapers and published in full in the provincial press, thus securing extraordinary attention for Ireland's case and my mission." He employed a local secretary, he writes, who translated for him sections of his speeches into Spanish, accenting them so that Ginnell could pronounce them "exactly as a Spaniard would." This won him many compliments: "In complimenting me, they always said that I had proved my distinct nationality by doing successfully what no English visitor had ever attempted. In the appeal to what is best in human nature, Ireland had unquestionably won."

Sectors of the Catholic Church provided support for his mission: "In response to a little circular issued by me in the Spanish language to Argentine parish priests, timidly suggesting a public requiem Mass in their respective churches on All Souls' Day, 1921, for the repose of the souls of those who had died for Ireland's independence, I received 65 replies, not alone favourable but enthusiastic, in some cases enclosing a printed leaflet which the priests themselves had issued, commending the purpose and inviting the attendance of their parishioners at the Mass and the sermon which they proposed to preach on the occasion. These leaflets were more strongly pro-Irish and anti-English than anything I had uttered abroad. The church that I attended on that occasion was richly draped in purple, with a bold white scroll overarching the sanctuary: 'Para las victimas de la tyrannia inglesa.' The sermon was exalted, noble, fearless, marked by passionate indignation, yet controlled by a majestic grace. Doctrine, logic and justice were frankly at one for Ireland's independence. On all such occasions, in every church, I was treated as the duly accredited representative of the Republic of Ireland, as such welcomed outside by the highest Church dignitaries, conducted by them on carpet from the street to the sanctuary, given the seat of honour there during the service, addressed from the pulpit by the preacher, and at the close conducted back with similar distinction; the choir playing the Argentine national anthem on my entrance and the 'Soldier's Song' on my departure."

While Ginnell did not succeed in his mission of winning recognition for the Irish Republic from any South American government, he gave a positive assessment of the prospects for such recognition: "Public opinion in South America was convinced that England, having called the truce in July, 1921, would find some way to save her face while letting Ireland go free rather than resume the war of extermination which had discredited her all over the world. The governments of all the South American republics were quite prepared to accord international recognition to the Republic of Ireland as soon as this could be done without incurring any unpleasant diplomatic consequences; and I was actually arranging a plan for having the recognition accorded by them all concurrently, which would enhance the effect while safeguarding individual states."[4]

Ginnell's assessment of the positive attitude among the governments of the region towards Irish independence may not be entirely fanciful. It is interesting to note, for example, the warm message sent by President Agusto B. Leguia of Peru on the establishment of the Free State: "Though widely sundered by land and sea, the news of the birth of the Irish Free State inevitably occasioned rejoicing in every generous heart throughout the Republic of Peru, remembering the gallant role which scores of Irishmen had played in the great battle of liberation in Hispanic-America a hundred years ago."[5] Meanwhile, on 26 April 1922, the Dáil was told that P.J. Little "has returned from an extensive tour in South Africa and South America" and that "Mr Lawrence Ginnell has completed a mission to Argentina and is returning home."[6] Unfortunately no details of the Little mission were given.

Diplomatic relations

Once established, however, the Irish state seems to have forgotten about Latin America though the Irish Argentines maintained their interest in Ireland as is evidenced, for example, by the group of Irish Argentine pilgrims who visited Dublin for the Eucharistic Congress in 1932. The initiative for establishing diplomatic relations also seems to have come from the Argentine side with the visit to Ireland in 1939 of Dr José E. Richards, a leading Irish-Argentine. He proposed the establishment of diplomatic relations but nothing was done until 1947 when an Irish commercial mission which went to Argentina to buy wheat also reached agreement on diplomatic relations. Already the issue had been mentioned in a letter in March 1945 from the secretary of the Department of External Affairs, Joseph Walshe, to the Irish Ambassador in Rome, Michael MacWhite, saying that after the war new missions would be opened first in Australia and New Zealand and then in Sweden, Argentina and Czechoslovakia. A chargé d'affaires represented Ireland in Buenos Aires from December 1947 until representation was upgraded to ambassador-level in early 1964. In 1957 the Minister for Defence, General Sean McEoin, visited Argentina for the celebrations marking the centenary of the death of Admiral William Brown.

The opening of relations with Argentina, however, had more to do with historical links with that country than with any new-found Irish interest in Latin America. It had to await the expansion of the Irish foreign service following EC membership in 1973 before relations were established with any other Latin American countries, beginning with Brazil in 1975, Mexico in 1977 and Venezuela in 1980. Relations with Brazil are handled through the Irish embassy in Lisbon, with Mexico through Washington and with Venezuela through Buenos Aires. Apart from formal diplomatic relations, Ireland also has honorary consuls in São Paulo and Rio de Janeiro, Lima, Quito, San Salvador and Mexico City. These are local business people with a limited diplomatic role and there is limited contol over them by the Department of Foreign Affairs in Dublin.

With the growing interest in Latin American issues among the Irish public in the 1980s pressure has increased to open more embassies in the region. Gerard Collins, Minister for Foreign Affairs between 1989 and 1992, says he "would like to see an upgrading of our diplomatic links with Latin America" but has to take account of budgetary constraints.[7] His two predecessors elaborated on the issue. Peter Barry, Minister for Foreign Affairs from 1982 to 1987 admitted that the lack of embassies in the region places Ireland "at a big disadvantage." He said that he considered moving Ireland's only embassy in Latin America from Buenos Aires to a more central location in the region which would facilitate extending diplomatic relations to more countries but that the Falklands/Malvinas war in 1982 made that impossible. "I would love to appoint more ambassadors," he said. "Obviously we should have one in Brazil and we should have one in Mexico covering the five Central American countries" but he cited economic reasons for not being able to open more.[8]

His successor, Brian Lenihan, Foreign Minister from 1987 to 1989 reiterated that "present constraints on public expenditure make the establishment of formal relations with other states in Latin America unlikely for the time being. The absence of formal relations does not preclude our having friendly relations with those states. There are contacts at the UN General Assembly in New York and elsewhere." He said that Ireland's involvement in European Political Co-operation (EPC) through which the twelve EC states seek to co-ordinate foreign policy positions, to some extent "compensates for our own less than complete network. For example, many of our partners have embassies in Central America and we have access to information through those channels."[9]

Irish policy on Latin America

As is reflected by its meagre diplomatic links with countries of the region, Irish foreign policy on Latin America also remains quite undeveloped. In the absence of an Oireachtas committee on foreign affairs, policy is often made in practice by diplomats directly dealing with issues which are not of great public interest which is the case with most issues relating to Latin America. An exception was the Irish stance on El Salvador and Nicaragua in the 1980s which, largely because of public concern about these countries and active lobbying by Irish solidarity groups, came to be more coherent and defined. Mr Collins acknowledged the public interest in Nicaragua and El Salvador throughout the last decade and added that this "obviously contributed to a greater focus on Central America and its problems, both at national level and in political co-operation with our EC partners."[10]

The broad principles underlying Irish policy on Latin America are a concern for democratisation and the rule of law, and interest in human rights. Action on these is now almost always taken in conjunction with EC partners through EPC. It would have to be a very exceptional situation for Ireland to take an independent initiative. The major example of such an independent Irish stand on a Latin American issue was during the Falklands/Malvinas war when, following Britain's sinking of the cruiser *Belgrano* outside the 200 mile exclusion zone around the islands, Ireland sought the removal of EC economic sanctions on Argentina. When it failed to get a unified EC decision, Ireland (together with Italy) broke ranks in refusing to continue with the sanctions, a stand warmly welcomed and still remembered in Argentina. Ireland also sought to convene a meeting of the UN Security Council to consider the situation but deferred this to allow the Secretary General continue his efforts to find a solution. While the Fianna Fáil MEP, Niall Andrews, who has taken an active interest in Latin American issues, claims that Ireland's action was "a development which arose out of a greater awareness about what was happening in Latin America"[11], most commentators considered it motivated more by the tense state of Anglo-Irish relations at the time.

Where Ireland has taken a particular interest in Latin America is on the issue of human rights. As a member of the UN Commission on Human Rights in Geneva from 1983-88, Ireland was among the most forceful of the EC countries in its concern for human rights. It has been particularly active on Guatemala, co-sponsoring motions condemning human rights abuses in that country. It strongly supported the extension of the mandate of the human rights rapporteur on Guatemala and did not co-sponsor a motion on that country in 1988 because it was not strong enough. Other Latin American countries about which Ireland expressed particular concern at the 1988 sessions of the Commission were Chile, El Salvador, Colombia, Paraguay, Peru and Haiti. Ireland resisted US pressure to censure human rights abuses in Cuba as it considered the pressure motivated more by US political hostility to Cuba than by a genuine interest in human rights. In a speech made at the 1988 session, the Irish Ambassador, Michael Lillis, outlined Ireland's view that "major social change in many parts of Latin America" was necessary before "we can be confident of the future of human rights and freedoms throughout Latin America." Ireland's stand on such issues has won it considerable praise and attention from human rights activists in some Latin American countries while it has been almost unknown at home.

The United Nations

At the United Nations also, Ireland has at times taken an active interest in Latin American issues. In his speech to the UN General Assembly in September 1981, the acting Minister for Foreign Affairs, Senator James Dooge, caused some controversy when he said Ireland accepted the principles underlying the Franco-Mexican Declaration which, the previous month, had recognised the Salvadorean opposition FDR-FMLN as a representative political force (see Chapter 11).

The Irish Ambassador to the UN from 1980 to 1983, Noel Dorr, was held in high regard by the Nicaraguan Foreign Minister at the time, Fr Miguel D'Escoto, because of the support given by Ireland in the early years of the Sandinista revolution. This was given added weight as Ireland was a member of the Security Council in 1981 and 1982. Mr Dorr was particularly active in seeking to find some ground for agreement between Nicaragua and the United States when, fearing a US invasion, Nicaragua brought the issue to the Security Council in March 1982. Consideration of the matter by the Security Council was opposed by the US Ambassador at the time, Jeane Kirkpatrick, who was President of the Council for that month and who argued it was rightly a matter for the Organisation of American States (OAS). While arguing strongly for negotiation between both countries in his speech to the Council, Mr Dorr also showed an understanding of the roots of civil unrest in Central America that was far from the understanding then vigorously promoted by Washington. It is worth quoting this section of the speech in full:

"We know that the immediate issue must be seen against the wider background of events in the region and of the upheaval which Nicaragua had to go through three years ago to rid itself of Somoza. Today several countries in Central America are in turmoil. In these countries highly stratified societies, structured on a grossly unequal basis, and maintained by repression, have crumbled, or are beginning to do so. Small nations, whose real need is peace and development, have been torn apart in civil strife as the violence built into unjust social structures over many generations takes a more open form, once these structures are openly challenged. Ruling elites react repressively in face of threats to their position and seek to maintain themselves against militant expressions of popular discontent. Death and injury have become commonplace and almost casual – not to say banal. Nicaragua went through just such an upheaval two years ago in ridding itself of the unjust and repressive Somoza regime. In El Salvador, and to a lesser extent in some other countries of the region, turmoil still continues." The Irish Ambassador's views of some close US allies or, in the case of Somoza, former allies must have caused more than a little annoyance in Washington.

Since 1989 Irish army officers have also for the first time participated in a UN operation in Latin America. This was the military observer mission in Central America, called ONUCA, set up in 1989. Its headquarters was in Tegucigalpa, the Honduran capital, but UN officers served in each of the five Central American countries. Three groups of Irish officers with twenty in each group have served consecutively on this mission which is due to terminate in March 1992.

Through European Political Co-operation

With the development of EPC over the 1980s, more and more does Ireland's policy find expression through this mechanism. According to diplomatic sources, within EPC Ireland takes an active interest in Latin American issues and in issues of particular concern to Latin America, for example the international debt crisis. An initiative on which Ireland took an active part in the mid-1980s was the development of the San José process through which an institutionalised relationship has been developed between the EC and the countries of Central America. It was under an Irish presidency that the founding meeting of this process took place in the Costa Rican capital in September 1984 with the delegation of EC foreign ministers led by the then Irish minister, Peter Barry. After France, Germany and Spain, Ireland is regarded by some diplomatic sources as the EC country which takes most interest in actively pushing this process along. This allows Ireland to have its concerns for democratisation and human rights expressed in ways that have more impact than if it acted unilaterally.

The main fora of the San José process are annual meetings of the EC and the Central American foreign ministers. The seventh such meeting was held in Dublin in April 1990, with the foreign ministers of the Central American countries and their colleagues from eight Latin American countries including Mexico, Brazil, Argentina, Colombia and Peru, in attendance. It was the largest meeting of Latin American ministers ever held in Ireland. These are the principal occasions at which EC concerns are voiced and, as is clear from the communiqué of the eighth meeting held in Managua in March 1991, these are not always wholeheartedly welcomed by the Central American ministers.

In dealing with agreements between government forces and guerrilla groups in countries of the region, the EC ministers added two concerns which appear only in their own name indicating the lack of agreement of the Central American ministers: an appeal to the governments of the region "to promote and develop the economic, social and security conditions necessary" to foster the integration of guerrilla forces into political life, and an appeal for "an end to any armed action against the civilian population." A paragraph welcoming the Salvadorean government's commitment to bring to justice those responsible for the murder of six Jesuits and their two helpers in

November 1989 also appears only in the name of the EC ministers. In this way, therefore, the San José process is establishing certain standards of behaviour and insisting that the governments of the region abide by them. Agreement on a programme of human rights for people in public office in Central America and especially those responsible for law, order and security indicates a practical way in which respect for human rights can be fostered.[12]

Apart from these meetings, the EC keeps an active watch on developments in Central America, issuing statements or making direct representation to regional governments as it thinks fit. For example, one issue it is monitoring is the treatment of street children in Guatemala while its decision to commission a report on the peace talks between the Salvadorean government and the FMLN indicates to both sides that the EC is keeping a close eye on the peace process. In this way, the EC hopes to foster reconciliation in Central America and to act quietly but effectively as a counterbalance to US influence. The Community also sees itself as providing a model of effective political and economic co-operation between countries which can stimulate a similar process in Central America. In this regard, the successes of the Esquipulas peace agreements within and between the Central American countries, the moves to establish a Central American parliament and the revamping of the Central American common market are all regarded as initiatives which the San José process has helped along. On the more negative side, some NGO sources have voiced fears that the process lends legitimacy to governments often unrepresentative of their peoples and may therefore not be in the best long-term interests of justice and lasting peace in the region. However, within its own terms, the process provides Ireland with a larger forum for diplomatic action than it would have on its own.

A more recent initiative taken under the Italian presidency of the EC in December 1990 is the dialogue with the Rio Group. Though begun in 1987, the Italian initiative put this dialogue on an altogether more enhanced footing making it a more ambitious initiative than even the San José process as it includes all the countries of Latin America with the smaller countries of Central America and the Caribbean being represented as regions having one seat each. Furthermore, the scale of the dialogue is greater as it is seen as a dialogue of equals not limited to issues of mutual concern. As such it is motivated by a concern of the Italians to help the Latin Americans to think of themselves as a region on the world stage. The significance has been underlined by an Irish diplomat, Philip McDonagh, working in the Latin American section of the EPC secretariat. In a paper read at a conference in Dublin, he said the dialogue with the Rio Group "confirms the existence of what we call the world stage, which is not something that has always been taken for granted. When as a Community we meet with the Rio Group, we are conscious not only of EC/Latin American relations but also of wider issues on which we hope to define a common approach."[13]

This Rio Group dialogue allows the Latin Americans to come as equal partners, bringing their particular viewpoint on world affairs. From his experience at ministerial meetings between both groups, Mr McDonagh spoke of "a fairly vigorous debate" taking place, "and one in which there were indeed elements of reciprocity."[14] Such a dialogue, he concluded, is best facilitated by allowing a certain freedom of conscience and of expression on both sides "from which we Europeans as well as others may have something to learn. A free and open dialogue implies a readiness to bring the internal affairs of one's own society into the diplomatic domain."[15]

An example of how Latin American concerns might influence EC thinking is in the position agreed on debt at the 1991 Luxembourg meeting between both groups. In this both sides agreed that the debt problem "was an obstacle to political, economic and social development and to stability and consolidation of democracy in the Latin American countries." They committed themselves to "co-operation between debtors and creditors in a spirit of joint responsibility" and recognised "the need for resolute action in the appropriate fora, the Club of Paris included."[16] (The Club of Paris is the forum where creditor governments meet to co-ordinate action on the debt and includes most EC governments though not Ireland.) Whether anything practical emerges from this remains to be seen but it does reflect the Community's readiness to accept the sense of urgency of the Latin Americans on the issue.

In these ways, Ireland is involved in developing new forms of regional co-operation with Latin America. It is significant that, partly due to the accession of Spain and Portugal to the EC in 1985, Community links with Latin America have greatly intensified since then. Both the San José process and the Rio Group dialogue are now the most ambitious forms of political co-operation between the EC and any regional groupings anywhere in the world. Though the seeds of both the Central American group and the wider Latin American group lie in local regional initiatives of the early 1980s, most notably the

Contadora initiative through which many of the larger Latin American countries sought to play a diplomatic role in resolving the Central American conflicts, EC involvement in supporting this initiative has greatly strengthened the process of Latin American regional integration. Such involvement by the Community acts as an important counterbalance to US interference, something greatly welcomed by the Latin Americans. From the point of view of Ireland's own policy on Latin America, however, involvement in EPC appears increasingly to substitute for an independent stand (see Chapter 11).

A Latin American view of Ireland's role

Ireland's major role is confirmed by the Mexican Ambassador to this country, Bernardo Sepúlveda. Based in London as he is also Ambassador to Britain, Mr Sepúlveda is well-placed to judge Ireland's role in the development of both the San José process and the Rio Group since he was his country's Foreign Minister from 1982-88. During this period Mexico played a key role both in seeking a diplomatic resolution of the Central American crisis and in fostering a common Latin American voice on these issues.

In an interview in the Mexican embassy in London,[17] Mr Sepúlveda spoke of Ireland's role during those years: "I can speak from my own experience. I would say that certainly Ireland played a very important role as an influence within the Community in the support we got, Latin America and Mexico particularly, that helped us establish a link between the Contadora process and Europe. The fact that we were able to convince the Community to hold periodic meetings with Contadora and with the San José process was an extremely important aspect of the peace process in Central America. And we always got very great support on the part of the Irish government." When asked how he evaluated Ireland's role on these issues vis-à-vis other EC countries, he replied: "Very high. From the very beginning, I certainly got a very clear and straightforward support on the part of the Irish government. The number of interviews I had with the Foreign Minister of Ireland were always very positive and encouraging. Not only with the Contadora process and the San José group but also when we established the Rio Group we always found the Irish government very supportive. The fact is that we have the sympathy of Ireland in creating these mechanisms of dialogue between Latin America and the European Community."

When asked whether Ireland represents within the Community the sort of position the Latin Americans would like to see represented, Mr Sepúlveda replied: "It has happened." When pressed to give an example other than the processes of regional co-operation already mentioned, he spoke of the agreement which had been recently negotiated and signed between the EC and Mexico. "This is what is called a third generation treaty for the Community and the contents of that treaty are very satisfactory. The fact is that we always got the support of Ireland."

The Ambassador characterised bilateral relations between Mexico and Ireland as "excellent" and said that in his period as Foreign Minister he instituted an annual meeting with his Irish counterpart at the UN General Assembly every September, a meeting which still takes place. As an example of how both countries share a similar outlook on many international issues, he said that "the pattern of voting at the UN is very similar."[18] He agreed that Mexico would find Ireland of more common mind than most of the Community countries. When asked whether Ireland has any distinctive contribution of its own to make on issues of concern to Latin America, the Ambassador mentioned that in the light of Mexico's negotiation of a free trade agreement with the United States, he planned to study the effects of the Anglo-Irish free trade agreement of 1965. "I would want to see what benefits Ireland gained out of that agreement. I also want to explore the advantages Ireland got out of its membership in the European Community," he said. When asked why he focused attention on Ireland, he replied: "Because it is a less developed country vis-à-vis Germany, the UK and France. I want to explore the benefits obtained by Ireland, Greece, Portugal and Spain."

Trade

While Ireland may be seen as taking an active political interest in Latin America through the European Community, this does not extend to trade relations. Ireland's exports to the Latin American and Caribbean region in 1989 were worth £171.3 million. Of this £83.6m, almost half of the total, was with Mexico. The next largest trade was with Brazil, worth £27m. Trade with all other countries in the region was negligible. The figure for 1990 was £155.1m, of which £80.3m was with Mexico and £41.8m with Brazil. This compares with £203.5m worth of exports to Africa and £496m to Asia. Only exports to Australasia, at £105m were less than those to Latin America. Imports from the region in 1989 were worth £122.5m and in 1990 £120.6m, indicating healthy trade balances in Ireland's favour in both years. (Ireland's overall exports in 1990 were worth £14.3 billion.)

Even this small amount of trade, however, exaggerates the extent of genuine Irish trading links with Latin America. This is illustrated by the case of Mexico, for example, which would appear to be a substantial trading partner. However, up to 80 per cent of the value of Ireland's exports to that country in the late 1980s was made up of milk powder which had been sold into EC intervention. In selling this to the Mexican government, therefore, Bord Bainne was effectively acting on behalf of the EC which subsidised the sale. The precarious nature of this trading link is illustrated by the fact that in 1991 the Mexican government had a surplus of milk powder and was not expected to be in a position to buy Irish milk powder. Exports to Mexico were therefore expected to slump dramatically. Fluctuations in Irish exports to Brazil, our second largest market in Latin America, are accounted for by the fact that most of these exports are made up of meat and meat products, again from intervention. Trade fluctuates according to Brazil's demand and also according to the amount of Irish meat in intervention in any given year. Ireland cannot therefore claim to have won markets in these countries; rather the bulk of our trade is due to the accidental fact that these countries need some products which Irish farmers have sold into intervention and the EC is willing to subsidise these sales.

Another factor inflating Irish exports to the region is the presence of foreign multinationals as a dominant sector of the Irish export trade. Thus exports of such products as chemicals or pharmaceuticals which, for example, accounted for the bulk of our exports to Argentina in 1990, are made up largely of the products of foreign multinational companies in Ireland. Again, these cannot be truly classed as markets won for Irish products as the market has really been developed by the multinationals and the fact that some of the products they sell there are made in Ireland is largely accidental.

An Bord Tráchtála, the semi-state body responsible for export promotion, admits that its policy in regard to Latin America and the Caribbean region is reactive rather than proactive. Where

Irish companies come to them interested in exporting to the region, the export board will facilitate them. But they do not go out to win markets for Irish products. This is partly due to the dismal economic condition of many of the region's countries where some Irish companies have had difficulty in getting paid for their products. Other factors inhibiting Irish companies are language, the small size of most Irish companies and the intense competition for markets.

A number of Irish multinational companies have, however, developed links with the region. The Jefferson Smurfit Group has subsidiaries manufacturing paperboard and packaging products in Colombia, Venezuela and Mexico which in 1990 accounted for 27 per cent of the group's worldwide sales and 37.5 per cent of its profits, the largest share of profits generated by any of the Group's regions. In Colombia the Group has been denounced for destroying the crops of indigenous peoples and expelling them from their land in the province of Cauca.[19]

The Shannon-based aircraft leasing company, Guinness Peat Aviation, has extensive business in Latin America and the Caribbean where it works with 23 airlines in 13 countries. Fruit Importers of Ireland had for many years been buying bananas from suppliers in a number of Latin American countries. In 1986 the company bought the US fruit importers, Fyffes, and now has direct links with suppliers in Belize, Surinam, Jamaica, the Windward Islands, Honduras and Ecuador, from which they supply British and European markets as well as the Irish market. They also have suppliers in Costa Rica, Panama, Colombia, Mexico and Guatemala. Another Irish company, Tuskar Resources, has been exploring for oil in Colombia.

As Latin American countries liberalise their economies and negotiate free trade deals with the United States, the Export Board is beginning to pay more attention to them as potential markets. The then Minister for Foreign Affairs, Gerard Collins, paid an official visit to Mexico in March 1991 during which he officially opened an Irish European Chamber of Commerce in Mexico, and he visited Brazil in January 1992. He sees possibilities for Irish exporters in markets such as Mexico, Brazil, Chile and Argentina. Mexico, through its new embassy in Dublin, is seeking to develop closer trading links. Venezuela is another country in which the export board sees potential. Meanwhile, Chile, recently returned to democracy and seeking to develop its trading links with the European Community, sent a semi-official trade mission to Ireland in June 1991 arguing that the historical contact between the two countries through

Bernardo O'Higgins provides a reason to develop both diplomatic and trading links. The export board and the Irish commercial sector seem cautious about these overtures, however.

The Labour TD, Michael D. Higgins, who has links with Latin America since his student days, thinks Ireland should develop trading links with the region more actively. "In a series of Latin American countries there is an enormous respect for Ireland and for Irish people," he said in an interview. "We have done really nothing to harness that. We have neglected the Latin American world entirely and this is quite outrageous despite the fact that even on crude right-wing commerical terms it is an enormous market. I also think that tourism is opening up there. I think our neglect is exposed there and I am very worried about that."[20]

Development aid

Latin America and the Caribbean receive relatively little attention from official development co-operation efforts. The bilateral aid programme, which accounts for a little under half of the Irish Official Development Assistance (ODA) budget, has concentrated on four priority African countries – Lesotho, Tanzania, Zambia and Sudan. This is justified by the fact that these are among the world's poorest countries and also mention is made of Irish missionary links and the fact that they are English-speaking. In its report on the bilateral programme in 1985, the Oireachtas Development Co-operation Committee recommended that the programme be extended and it mentioned three Latin American countries as suitable for inclusion – Brazil, Chile and Nicaragua. However, with cutbacks in ODA such an extension is not likely in the foreseeable future. As Mr Collins put it: "Since our bilateral aid programme is a small one in volume terms, it is preferable to concentrate the aid in a small number of countries to achieve maximum effect and impact rather than spread it over a larger number of countries."[21]

The other main channel through which official Irish aid reaches developing countries is the multilateral programme which constitutes a little over half the total ODA. This is made up of payments, usually mandatory, to international organisations of which Ireland is a member, the EC and the UN in particular. Ireland has, however, no say on where its contribution to these programmes is spent so it is impossible to determine what percentage of it ends up in Latin America. The EC's main development co-operation programme is the Lomé

Convention with sixty-seven African, Caribbean and Pacific (ACP) states. Ireland has taken a particular interest in this programme and the first three conventions were signed under Irish presidencies of the EC. Lomé IV was signed in December 1989 and is to run for ten years. Ireland contributes to the European Development Fund which is the source of financing for the Lomé Convention.

Latin America and the Caribbean do, however, benefit in small ways under a number of headings in the ODA programme. A co-financing scheme, under which the Department of Foreign Affairs co-finances projects with Irish agencies, earmarks some funds for Latin America. Under this heading, the amount given to projects in Latin American countries increased from £11,130 in 1988 for projects in Panama and El Salvador to £45,365 in 1991 for projects in Brazil, El Salvador and Peru. Other countries to benefit in recent years include Paraguay, Nicaragua and Chile. A number of students from Latin America and the Caribbean also receive fellowships to study in Ireland under an education and training scheme while the state-funded Agency for Personal Service Overseas (APSO) every year funds a number of Irish people to work in Latin America and the Caribbean. A further heading under which Latin America receives some Irish aid funds is the emergency disaster relief fund. This allocated £50,000 to Peru in 1990 and a further £20,000 in 1991.

As with the bilateral aid programme, however, African countries tend to benefit most under these schemes also. The same is true of two other state-assisted agencies, DEVCO, the state agencies' development co-operation organisation and HEDCO which creates links between third level institutions in Ireland and those in developing countries. Only a very minor part of these two agencies' work is in Latin American or Caribbean countries.

Footnotes

1. Gerard Collins TD in written answers to questions supplied by the author, August 1991
2. Dáil Éireann, Official Report for 17 August 1921, Dublin, Stationery Office, pp 16,17
3. Ibid.
4. Quotes from Labhras MagFhionnghail (Lawrence Ginnell) 'A Glance Back at the Time of our Harmony' in *The Catholic Bulletin*, 1922, pp 768-770
5. Text given in William S. Fitz-Gerald, ed., *Voice of Ireland*, Dublin, John Heywood Ltd., 1924, p 70
6. Dáil Éireann, Official Report for 26 April 1922, p 238
7. Gerard Collins TD, op. cit.
8. Peter Barry TD in an interview with the author, March 1988
9. Brian Lenihan TD in written answers to questions supplied by the author, March 1988
10. Gerard Collins TD, op. cit.

11. Niall Andrews MEP in an interview with the author, March 1988
12. See the joint political declaration of the Managua Ministerial Conference between the European Community and the countries of Central America and Panama, 18-19 March 1991
13. Philip McDonagh, 'Reflections on European Political Co-operation', a paper given at a conference on Neutrality and European Political Co-operation, held in Dublin, 7 May 1991, p 15
14. Ibid., p 19
15. Ibid., p 20
16. See the Conclusions of the first Institutionalised Ministerial Meeting between the European Community and the Rio Group, Luxembourg 26-7 April 1991
17. These and following quotes are taken from the author's interview with Bernardo Sepúlveda, April 1991
18. Ireland's voting record at the UN is closer to that of Scandinavian and some European neutral countries such as Austria than it is to that of the larger EC countries. (See Michael Holmes, Nicholas Rees, and Bernadette Whelan *Irish Foreign Policy and the Third World*, Trócaire and Gill & Macmillan, Dublin to be published 1992.) Mexico would tend to take a similar position.
19. See 'Smurfit destroyed crops, say Colombian Indians', in *The Sunday Tribune*, 17 December 1989, p A4
20. Michael D. Higgins TD in an interview with the author, March 1988
21. Gerard Collins TD, op. cit.

Chapter 10

Forging Links: The Irish Church and Latin America

"I don't think now that I would be able to deal with the Irish situation as it is at the moment had I not experienced the kind of Church that I experienced over there [in Latin America]."

– Bishop Michael Murphy of Cork and Ross[1]

If the Irish state has shown little interest in Latin America and the Caribbean, closer links have been forged since the 1950s by Irish missionaries. Though the overall number of Irish missionaries in the region has been small compared to the numbers working in Africa and Asia, their presence generated an interest among Irish people in countries of the region which in the 1980s flowered into active concern at home about developments in El Salvador and Nicaragua. The influence of such concern was dramatically seen during the visit to Ireland of the US President Ronald Reagan in June 1984 which was dominated by widespread protests at US policies in Central America (and also that country's policy on armaments and on the Philippines). Apart from this, returning missionaries have had an impact on the Irish Catholic Church as they seek to promote here the new model of "popular Church" to the development of which they have actively contributed in Latin America.

Legion of Mary

Apart from Irish priests and religious who went to work in Latin America in growing numbers from the 1950s onwards, an early Irish missionary endeavour involved lay people who were sent to Latin America to establish the Legion of Mary. For the highly clericalised and rather moribund Latin American Catholic Church at the time, this was a novel concept. It not only involved lay people actively in Church activities but, unlike other lay groups such as Acción Católica which was also being introduced to Latin America at the time, it gave to lay people rather than to priests the power of decision-making. It thus can be seen as one of the influences promoting a more central role for lay people, one of the essential elements of what was later to flower into the new model of "popular Church" which has become perhaps the most dynamic and far-reaching renewal movement in the Catholic Church worldwide in the 1970s and 1980s.

Seamus Grace was thirty years old when the Legion asked him to go with Alfie Lamb to Bogotá in July 1953. Though the Legion was already established in a small way, he remembers being unhappy with some of its activities.[2] He mentions, for example, that Legionaries were concentrating on such work as taking a census of the Catholic population rather than getting out into the barrios to work directly with the poor and get them involved in the Legion's work.

From Bogotá, the work extended out to many parts of Colombia. The system used was similar to that developed by the Legion in Ireland at the time. Called team extension, this involved setting up a number of *praesidia* (Legion branches) in an area and entrusting to these new members the establishment of further *praesidia* in that area. The Irish envoys involved the Colombian Legionaries from the beginning in spreading the Legion around their own country. Seamus Grace led the way in visiting bishops and getting their permission to set up in their dioceses. They were not used to lay people coming to them like that, he remembers, but adds: "They were prepared to listen and eventually gave permission and often their enthusiastic support." Once he got his permission, he would go to a place, make contacts in whatever way he could and establish a few *praesidia*. He would then move on, leaving the work in the hands of the local people and return three months later to see how it had advanced. Usually the people he left in charge were poor and often illiterate yet on returning he would find the work advancing. In this way the Legion "mushroomed" around Colombia, he says.

Seamus Grace remembers the "total inertia in the Latin American Church at the time." Areas, including large towns, had been without priests for many years and the bishops encouraged the Legion to go to these areas. He remembers going to the town of Buenaventura with a population of 30,000 which had no priest for five years, or, when he moved on to Venezuela, being asked to go to the city of San Fernando de Apure which, under Masonic influence, had run all priests out of town. Yet, even in such unlikely places, he managed to make contacts with local people on whom he could rely to establish Legion *praesidia*.

"We never met hostility among the poor, prisoners, the neediest," says Seamus Grace. It was among the poor, therefore, that the Legion flourished but there was also a good social mix. "There were gifted generous people who were good leaders," he says. He established successful *praesidia* in prisons in Colombia and Venezuela "where every member was in for murder." The conditions in these prisons were Dickensian, he says, but the Legion's success was based on the fact that the prisoners "wanted people to come to talk to them as human beings. This was a unique experience. They were not getting lectures, just a chat. We got a huge welcome." They also went into leper colonies where the Legion established *praesidia* among the lepers which helped them to help one another. "We didn't limit ourselves to those with even a minimal education," he says. "We found they were capable of nearly everything."

Seamus Grace singles out the region's papal nuncios at the time for particular praise. Many of them he says were working to build a stronger and more vibrant Church and gave the Legion particular support. Among moves afoot at the time were the first efforts to bring the Latin American bishops together as a group to look at their problems. This was to lead to the establishment of the Conference of Latin American Bishops (CELAM) in 1955 and Seamus Grace was present at a preliminary meeting in 1954. He was probably the only non-American or non-Hispanic to speak at that meeting, he recalls.

From Colombia, Seamus Grace moved on to Venezeula bringing with him a number of Colombians. Meanwhile Alfie Lamb had moved southwards, to Ecuador. Between them, they established the Legion in almost all the countries of Latin America over subsequent years. From Venezuela, Seamus Grace went to El Salvador, Costa Rica, Nicaragua, Guatemala, Honduras, Panama and Mexico. He got as far as southern Texas before returning to Ireland in 1956. Alfie Lamb went from Ecuador to Peru, Bolivia, Brazil, Uruguay and Argentina where he died of cancer in January 1959 at the age of twenty-six. The cause for his canonisation has been formally initiated and is now being processed both in Latin America and in Ireland. Other Irish Legionaries followed, among them Mary Clerkin, Tadhg McMahon, Noel Lynch, Louis O'Neill, Una Twomey and Dick Maher. The Legion of Mary soon put down deep roots in Latin America and established itself as one of the major lay movements of the Church there at that time.

The Legion is often criticised for not having devoted sufficient attention to social issues. But, as Seamus Grace points out "what it did for the dignity of the poorest and the neediest and in crossing social barriers in Latin America was quite an achievement." Its impact on subsequent developments in the Latin American Church is much harder to assess. However, links can be traced as, for example, in the contacts Seamus Grace had with Archbishop Chavez of San Salvador, the predecessor of Archbishop Romero and the man whose pastoral vision helped to develop a lay leadership in the Salvadorean Church which led to the flowering of basic christian communities and christians active in the struggle for justice.

During his travels in Latin America, Seamus Grace met some Irish American priests but he met no Irish ones. When he returned to Ireland, therefore, he visited many Irish orders urging them to send members to work in Latin America. He remembers visiting the Columbans, the Holy Rosary sisters, the Medical Missionaries of Mary, the Redemptorists and the Divine Word Missionaries. "Few people knew anything about Latin America at the time," he recalls. When he told them of his success in establishing the Legion, "it was unbelievable to people that things like this could happen in Latin America. The attitude was that the Church was dead, decadent. Nobody expected anything to come from it."

The Irish missionary movement in Latin America

There was a small Irish missionary presence in the region from the middle of the 19th century with, for example, the Mercy sisters and the Passionist and Pallotine Fathers serving the Irish community in Argentina (see Chapter 8) and the Irish Dominicans and Holy Ghost Fathers in Trinidad (who had been preceded there by a large number of Irish diocesan priests). These missions, however, had arisen for specific reasons: to serve the Irish in Argentina and virtually establish an Irish-style Catholic Church for them there and, in the case of Trinidad, as a result of the British colonial presence. They followed the pattern of the Irish missionary movement elsewhere in the last century – following the Irish diaspora or British colonisation. With few Irish in Latin America and the British colonial presence limited to the Caribbean, it was not surprising that the growing Irish missionary movement in the early 20th century paid the region little attention. Ireland was of course not unique in this. For missionary societies throughout Europe at the time, Latin America was not considered mission territory; not only had it been evangelised in the 15th and 16th centuries but it had its own diocesan structures and a largely native clergy.

The foundation of the Maynooth Mission to China (later known as the Columban Fathers) in 1916 marks "the great watershed in the history of the modern Irish missionary movement", according to an historian of that movement, Dr Edmund M. Hogan.[3] Yet from the beginning it also marked a break with the nature of the Irish movement up to then and dedicated itself exclusively to mission to non-christians. It also made an explicit decision not to work in Africa, possibly because that was then a favoured destination for Irish missionaries. The single most important group in the Irish missionary movement therefore sent its members to Asian countries exclusively; it was only following the Chinese Revolution in 1949 and with the advance of other communist movements in Korea and Indochina creating a sombre prospect for the future of Irish missionary work in the region that attention was turned to Latin America.

With the numbers of Columbans growing very fast, new outlets for them had to be found. In 1950, the Columban superior general sent a priest to Latin America to look at possibilities and as a result the Columban Fathers opened parishes in Lima, Peru, and Santiago, Chile, in 1951-52 and sent two priests to staff the Apostleship of the Sea in Buenos Aires, Argentina. Though the Columban parishes in Peru and Chile are still flourishing, they account for a relatively small number of Columbans in comparison to those serving in Asian countries and it was only as recently as 1986 that new missions in Latin America and the Caribbean were opened when Columbans were sent to Brazil, Jamaica and Belize for the first time. As the Columban historian, Fr Michael O'Neill puts it: "For many years after 1950 the Latin American mission was regarded by most Columbans as peripheral to the main missionary thrust of their Society."[4]

It was only following an initiative begun by Pope Pius XII and furthered with greater resolve by Pope John XXIII following his election in 1958 that Latin America became widely considered a mission territory. The Pope appealed to superiors of religious orders and to individual hierarchies to send priests to serve in Latin America. In December 1960, he wrote to the Irish bishops asking them to facilitate Irish priests to serve with the Columbans in Latin America.

This papal interest in Latin America had most impact in the

United States. There, religious groups had been asked in a speech in 1961 to send 10 per cent of their membership to serve in Latin America within ten years, a speech that is regarded by one historian of the US missionary movement, Gerald M. Costello, as "one of the most significant in the history of the US Church."[5] In Ireland, the impact was less immediate though the new interest generated in Latin America led to a number of orders sending men within the following years: the Redemptorists to Brazil in 1960, the Kiltegans (though founded to work in Africa) also to Brazil in 1963, the Dominicans to Argentina in 1965, the Holy Ghosts to Brazil in 1967 and the Franciscans to Chile and El Salvador in 1968. Diocesan priests from Dublin, Meath and Armagh also began to serve in small numbers with the Columbans in Peru and Chile while a number of those working with the Kiltegans also came from dioceses in Ireland.

Meanwhile as the changes in the Latin American Church attracted more and more attention, so did more Irish orders take an interest in sending members to work there. For sisters in particular it provided an opening for direct pastoral work and more personal initiative, living among the poor in shanty towns and working alongside them to build a new model of Church at the service of a new society of justice. This differed from the sort of missionary work which still predominated in Asia and Africa – running schools and hospitals. In Latin America also they found a hierarchy more open to the aspirations of the Second Vatican Council. Throughout the 1970s, 1980s and into the 1990s therefore groups of sisters have gone in small numbers from many Irish congregations to open houses among the poor in different parts of Latin America.

As a result, Latin America is the only part of the world in which numbers of Irish missionaries are growing though overall numbers are still relatively small. In 1990, 4,498 Irish Catholic missionary personnel were working in developing countries, 63 per cent of them in Africa, 22 per cent in Asia and Oceania and 14.5 per cent in Latin America and the Caribbean. Yet, though the total number of Irish missionaries working overseas declined from 7,085 in 1965 to 4,498 in 1990 the numbers working in Latin America increased from 585 in 1965 to 655 in 1990. The Irish missionaries in Latin America are also spread widely. In 1990, Irish Catholic missionaries were working in 24 Latin American and Caribbean countries. The largest number, 195, were in Brazil, with 108 in Peru, 62 in Trinidad, 61 in Chile, 54 in Argentina, 38 in Ecuador, 22 in Venezuela, 15 in Mexico, 15 in Grenada, 13 in El Salvador, 12 in Paraguay and smaller numbers in the Bahamas, Belize, Bolivia, Colombia, Costa Rica, Guatemala, Haiti, Jamaica, Nicaragua, St Lucia, St Vincent, Uruguay and the Virgin Islands. This Irish presence is by far the most extensive of any Irish presence in the region.

Cork mission to Peru

It was in Cork that Pope John's appeal was to have its most significant impact on the Irish Church. Here Bishop Lucey had established a relationship with Cardinal Cushing of Boston who helped fund the building of churches in Cork. When the cardinal visited in 1961, he asked Bishop Lucey to send some Cork priests to serve in Peru with the Missionary Society of St James which he had established in 1958. One of the three sent by Bishop Lucey was the man who was to succeed him as Bishop of Cork, Dr Michael Murphy.

He vividly recalls the conditions he encountered in the rural town of Abancay at 9,000 feet in the Andes of Peru when he arrived to work there in 1962.[6]

"The physical distances were enormous, the main means of travel was horseback or walking and there was only one road, a dirt road connecting Cusco with Abancay. When you went off that 'highway' you could ride for three or four hours to get to a place. There was nothing romantic about riding the horses for four or five hours up the mountains and down the mountains. I do not know how we escaped being killed by being thrown from the horses. I would stay overnight and the conditions were terrible. There was one place where I stayed and the guy who looked after the goats grazing outside the church had to look after the *cura* when he came. He would have to get the soup, and that is all you would get, and there was very little interesting about it as the water was never boiled. Anyway I slept there where they kept the mule; he swept it out and I went in with my sleeping bag. You always had visions of the missions being tough but this was tougher. You were inside this place with only a door and no window for air and you would get a thousand fleas in the bag with you. They were the most vicious fleas and would wake you up eating you. In the morning the barking dogs would wake you and you felt awful because you were tired due to the altitude and then breakfast was only a crust of bread. So it was quite an experience, very raw.

"I had never experienced anything like it before. You had

mass perhaps once a month [in the different villages]. You were doing good if you could get in a bit of instruction and train a few catechists. It was an extraordinary situation because it would have been much easier if they were all pagans and unbaptised. But there they were all baptised or we presumed they were. The bishop went out to show me the ropes. He was Peruvian, half Indian and spoke Quechua. He must have had about 40 or 50 marriages [that day] and I don't know how many baptisms. There were no pre-matrimonial papers of any kind. I was amazed at this. Then we married the couples and baptised their kids.

"The way I would describe the Church I found in that place at that time is to say it was in the gutter. There was some respect for the bishop but the ordinary priest was used. He had to show up for the *fiesta*, he had to say masses. But he was very badly educated and very poor, basically a peasant. He had to have a little business on the side and he had a few kids too. We came in and we were different, independent and had money. So for the people it was a culture shock. We were always exposed to the accusation from the left at local level that we were agents of American imperialism. These people were sharp enough. I often heard Radio Moscow broadcasting in Quechua to the people."

One of the lessons Bishop Murphy learned from his three years in Abancay is that such difficult missions are for trained and life-long missionaries. Therefore when Bishop Lucey asked him and his companion, Fr Michael Crowley, to look for a more permanent mission place in Peru for the Cork diocese, it was along the coast they looked where conditions were a little easier. In 1965 together with Bishop Lucey who was on a visit to Peru, they chose the northern coastal city of Trujillo, Peru's second largest city with a population of around 500,000. Founded in 1536, it was one of the first cities established by the Spaniards after they conquered the Inca empire and the city's many colonial churches testify to the traditional nature of the Church there. What they found surrounding the city were growing shanty towns with a population of around 40,000 but with virtually no Church presence. It was in these areas that they decided to establish the Cork mission to Peru.

It was a far-seeing move for what were then the two small suburbs of El Porvenir and Esperanza have grown into large shanty towns which now spread out in a semicircular arc in the desert surrounding the city. They are now home to some

400,000 people, over half the city's population, most of them people who have moved from the rural villages of the Andes seeking a better life. The four parishes staffed by the priests of the Cork diocese (with some associates from Kerry) serve a population larger than the whole of the dioceses of Cork and Ross. As well as around twelve Irish priests, Bons Secours and Mercy sisters from Cork ran schools and health centres in the parishes.

The Cork mission, served by priests and sisters from Cork and maintained by the donations of Cork people, bore the identity of its origin more than do most missionary endeavours. This was partly because, unlike most missionaries, the Cork priests go to Peru to serve for a limited term and then return home. It is not surprising therefore that their approach was very much influenced by the way things are done in Cork. This is mirrored in the cluster of church buildings which serve each parish – church, priests' and sisters' houses, schools and health centres. Indeed the similarity is visible even in the design of the ultra-modern circular church for the Madre de Cristo parish which was first intended for Carrignabhear in Co. Cork. The work too was similar to what they would be doing in Cork – providing religious services, administering schools, visiting the people.

Influenced, however, by pastoral developments elsewhere in Peru, the priests had also begun to move into less institutional work and could be found, for example, helping people to raise rabbits or guinea pigs to supplement their meagre income. With the worsening economic situation in Peru in the late 1980s, the Cork mission decided to open food kitchens for the local people and collected £250,000 in two weeks in Cork which allowed sixty food kitchens be set up. Similarly, instead of giving all religious instruction in the schools or churches they were adopting the Latin American system of family catechesis, forming lay catechists who bring the parents together in small groups in each others' homes and educate them to educate their children. Elsewhere in Latin America this approach has resulted in the growth and flourishing of basic christian communities. Bishop Murphy is also keen that the social gospel be preached forcefully and points to the fact that Cork priests and sisters have marched with strikers and been exposed to gunfire as evidence that this was being done. He mentions that he has received letters accusing some of his priests of being communists.

In late 1991, life in the Cork mission was rudely shattered when Sendero Luminoso guerrillas (see Chapter 6) took over the medical centre in the parish of El Porvenir as it was crowded with local people. They took £1,000 worth of drugs and painted slogans on the walls threatening the Cork priests whom they called "Irish imperialists." As an Australian nun, two Polish priests and an Italian priest had been murdered by Sendero Luminoso in the previous months, the threats against the Cork personnel were taken very seriously. In January 1992, Bishop Murphy announced that eight of the twelve Cork priests were withdrawing from Peru, four to go to Chile and four to return home and that two of the four parishes were being handed back to the Archbishop of Trujillo to staff. The Irish Bons Secours sisters have withdrawn to Ecuador while a group of Mercy sisters returned to Ireland.

Thus the handover to Peruvian personnel that was being planned has happened under unforeseen circumstances. After twenty-five years, the mission was preparing local Peruvians to take over. The Mercy and Bons Secours communities were made up mostly of Peruvian sisters and a number of Peruvians were also being trained for the priesthood under the supervision of a Cork priest, one of whom has been ordained. This now leaves local people better prepared to continue the work in the four parishes.

An indirect result of the Cork mission to Peru came through Fr Michael Crowley, one of the priests who helped establish it. As chaplain in University College Cork in the early 1970s, he became friendly with a young woman from the United States, Jean Donovan, who was studying in the College during the academic year 1973-74. He shared with her his love for Latin America so that when she returned to Cleveland she volunteered for her local diocesan mission to El Salvador. There she worked in the coastal town of La Libertad, less than an hour's drive from the capital, San Salvador. In September 1980, she returned to visit friends in Cork; three months later she was murdered by members of the Salvadorean military together with three US sisters in a crime that shocked international public opinion. Every year since 1984 an annual Jean Donovan lecture has been given at UCC by a visiting authority on Latin America, a meeting which has established itself as Ireland's foremost occasion for diplomats, academics, missionaries, journalists and interested members of the public to debate Latin America.

Reverse mission: impact on the Irish Church

Irish interest in the new developments transforming the Latin American Church began to manifest itself from the late 1960s. Fr

Ireland and Latin America

Michael O'Neill of the Columbans remembers the controversy caused when he put a photograph of a Brazilian nun giving out Communion on the cover of the March 1968 issue of *The Far East* magazine of which he was then editor. In the Irish Church at the time this was considered far too radical but Fr O'Neill wrote with foresight in his editorial in that issue: "Perhaps it is not all that inconceivable that you might eventually be receiving Holy Communion from a nun in your home parish."[7] Though a small example, this indicates how the Latin American Church opened hitherto unconsidered possibilities for Irish Catholics at the time.

More substantial was the first conference in Ireland on liberation theology which was organised by an Irish Jesuit, Fr Michael O'Sullivan in 1976. He says that the Latin American Church was "an important guide" for him and a number of his Jesuit confreres. "We saw in Latin America how to be a Church relevant to reality, to have an option for the poor and a thrust for social justice."[8] The following February he joined with a group of lay Christians of different denominations to found an Irish branch of Christians for Socialism, a movement first established in Chile during the Allende government. The group, which issued a public call to Irish Christians to vote for socialist candidates in the 1977 general election, "brought faith and social justice together", says Fr O'Sullivan. Rather more tame was the conference organised by the Irish Theological Association in January 1977 on liberation theology which had Dr Garret FitzGerald as one of its principal speakers!

Meanwhile, among the growing number of Irish priests and sisters working in Latin America, many of them very actively participating in the radical changes reshaping the Church there, were some concerned to shake up the Church back at home. Yet, apart from the diocese of Cork which has had its unique institutional link with Peru, the impact has happened more through the individual work of priests or sisters who have returned from Latin America with a new pastoral vision than through any coherent movement or group. This is partly because many have found great difficulty translating back into the highly institutional and clerical Irish Church the more community-based approaches they developed in Latin America with the active involvement of lay people. They return from Latin America often fired by their experience of a Church to the forefront of the struggle for social justice to re-insert themselves in a Church back home more concerned about the times for evening mass and confession. The culture shock on return has been enormous for some. Fiodhna Callanan, who worked with Viatores Christi in Venezuela for four years, observes that priests who return from Latin America "need energy to sustain them over a long period. They very much work as individuals, there is no networking going on. People who have a wider vision are sucked into day-to-day duties and a tiredness sets in."[9]

Changing parish life

Yet many have recovered from that to adapt their Latin American experience to working in an Irish parish. This usually involves an attempt to encourage lay people to participate more in parish life, to link faith more to the real concerns of people's lives and to develop an interest in issues of social justice at home and abroad. An interesting initiative taken by the Dominicans in 1990 has been to send three priests, two of whom have worked in Argentina and one in Trinidad, to staff a new parish with some 80 per cent unemployment in Ballybeg, Waterford, with the express intention of "encouraging the empowering of the local people," according to the Dominican provincial, Fr Tom Jordan OP.[10] The example of Latin America has also inspired some Jesuits in the attempts to develop a new model of parish life in such places as Gardiner Street in Dublin's inner city or in Ballymun. Two new small Jesuit communities in Dublin are named after Jesuits martyred in Latin America in the recent past: Luis Espinal House in Gardiner Place after Fr Luis Espinal tortured and killed by the military in Bolivia in 1980, and Rutilio Grande community in the Ballymun flats after Fr Rutilio Grande killed by the Salvadorean military in 1977.

Significantly the diocese of Cork and Ross is the one Irish diocese making a concerted attempt to implement a process of pastoral planning and the active participation of lay people in Church life both at diocesan level and in each parish. It cannot be unrelated that it is the diocese with the largest number of priests who have served in Latin America – about a quarter of the total number of priests in the diocese, including the bishop. Bishop Murphy sees "an inevitability about it having an influence over the long haul and more and more so. I think that they should certainly be more open to change and less fearful."[11] As part of the pastoral planning process, Bishop Murphy appointed a Social Care Commission, made up mostly of lay people, which in 1984 reported on how the diocese can more effectively respond to the needs of four groups: the family, the elderly, youth and the unemployed. In a document setting out his vision of the parish in 1986, Bishop Murphy wrote: "In the past, there was a lot of passivity among our people. They expected – and it was the rule – that the priest would lead, do, and control everything. That must change. The key to the building of this new parish community is participation by the people. I speak of real participation, the giving of responsibility to the people of the parish...This participation must be broadened out into every area of parish life. The parish must be a place where lay leadership is inspired, and lay initiative supported."[12] The process of pastoral planning is an attempt to plan a process to achieve this goal which, if achieved, would herald a revolution in the Irish Church every bit as far-reaching as has happened in the Latin American Church.

Bishop Murphy brings back to his work in Ireland valuable insights learned in Latin America. Indeed he says: "I don't think that I would be able to deal with the Irish situation as it is at the moment had I not experienced the kind of Church that I experienced over there."[13] He cites two examples. One relates to the changes happening in Ireland and their impact on the Church. "The Irish situation for priests and bishops is quite difficult at the moment. Some people are a bit demoralised, especially older people who lived with a certain kind of Church. On the other hand I think it is better off when we are at a distance from the state." He says he is able to appreciate the positive aspects of this new situation in Ireland because he lived in Latin America in a Church "very much on the periphery." This contrasted with the Church he had known in Ireland, he says, which was "powerful and dominant". He adds: "I think there is always a danger in that situation because power is a very dangerous thing and it is very easy to abuse it."

His second example concerns partnership between clergy and laity. "I think we have got to be able to listen to what people are saying. One of the things that saddens me is the sense that lay people are not trusted. After all the powerful influence we've had if we can't trust the people then we've failed." Overall, Bishop Murphy senses a "weariness among some in the Irish Church. The danger is that we might 'miss the boat'. We still have a great opportunity here but time is running out. There is risk involved but we have to consider what we are risking and the risk we are taking by not taking a risk."

As well as the impact on parish life, many religious orders are finding searching questions about their life and mission being asked by those members who have been in Latin America. Priests who served in Latin America have had a "disproportionate impact on the Columbans back home", says Fr O'Connell, director of the Irish region.[14] A Columban who worked in Peru for twenty years, Fr Noel Kerins, says that "the massive poverty and dehumanisation in Lima posed the question of what does it mean to be a Christian. Part of the Church in Lima was trying to respond to that question."[15] As similar questions are beginning to be asked with ever greater insistence in Ireland, the experiences of those who have in some way been touched by the transformations in the Latin American Church become ever more relevant.

Applying Freire's methods

A number of other initiatives have developed through which the vision of those returned from abroad, some from Latin America, is having a more sustained impact in Ireland. Two of these date from 1981 when the first Partners in Mission course began and when the Dublin Institute for Adult Education and the Irish Missionary Union ran a workshop on basic christian communities. The Partners in Mission brought together six priests, six sisters and six lay people all of whom had worked abroad, with the same numbers who had worked at home. Using educational methods developed by the Brazilian educationalist Paulo Freire, they sought to develop a more critical faith linked to a more critical understanding of the social and political situation in Ireland so as to encourage more radical action for change. Partners in Mission has developed over the years and now employs two fulltime staff, of whom Fiodhna Callanan is one, who work with groups around the country particularly in disadvantaged areas.

The workshop on basic communities has developed in a different way, leading to the establishment of a programme of parish renewal in the Dublin diocese which has established three priorities: developing structures of lay participation, the renewal of priests and outreach to youth. Since 1988, this employs six people, four of them lay people. As part of this process, a Brazilian team which works to develop basic communities throughout Latin America and led by a well-known priest, Fr José Marins, has visited Ireland three times to work with groups, many of them from disadvantaged areas.

The early enthusiasm has also given way to a more serious attempt to face the difficulties of implementing these approaches in Ireland. Fiodhna Callanan says that after ten years Partners in

Mission is now grappling with these; she finds in Ireland, for example, a great resistance to spending time trying to identify the root causes of problems through discussing and listening to one another. People see this as a waste of time and urge instead that some action should be undertaken. She also finds in Ireland that "a lot of personality differences, power struggles, personal agendas are put onto the political agenda and take over."[16] Introducing a christian dimension is also a great difficulty in Ireland unlike in Latin America, she finds: "When people talk about the Church they get very, very angry and others get very defensive." In many cases Irish groups with which she works do not want the christian dimension introduced, she says.

Fr Ciaran Earley OMI, who worked in Brazil and now works with the parish renewal programme in the Dublin diocese, finds a sense of mission lacking here in Ireland. "The Church is not formed to have a mission. Past experiences of guilt and of authoritarianism are very hard to overcome."[17] Another dimension he finds lacking in Ireland is a systematic reflection on our own reality similar to what has been done in Latin America. Fr Michael O'Sullivan SJ, who worked in Chile from 1982-4, agrees. "Not enough has been done to get people together to reflect on their own reality," he says.[18] Without this no distinctively Irish theology can emerge to inform the growth of a new model of Church here.

Another development of the 1980s which, if not directly influenced by the Latin American experience is inspired by it, has been the emergence of a radical critique of government social and economic policy by Church groups such as the Conference of Major Religious Superiors, the Catholic Social Service Conference and the Jesuit Centre for Faith and Justice. Through pre-budget submissions and post-budget analyses in particular, these have shown up the true priorities of government spending and the lack of a real will to tackle poverty and unemployment. The voice of such groups is weakened, however, by the fact that other sectors of the Church, most notably certain bishops, offer a far more muted critique of government policy or even at times echo government criticisms of this "poverty lobby". It is a point to which Bishop Murphy of Cork refers when he says he thinks there should be "much closer co-operation between religious and bishops. I think there should not be two voices. There is no question in my mind of what the Church should be saying. The question is what should the Church be doing."[19]

The image of the Latin American Church continues to exercise a fascination for Irish people. Fr John O'Connell of the

Columbans says that of people with a missionary vocation in Ireland over the past ten years, "if given an option 90 per cent would go to Latin America."[20] He adds that "all lay missionaries want to go to Latin America because they see the Church there as being more vibrant, more socially involved and more participative." That, of course, says as much about what sort of Church many of the most committed people in the Irish Catholic Church want, as it says about the Latin American Church itself. In many ways what these people have to offer back home when they return may be as important as what they offer to those in Latin America with whom they work.

Footnotes

1. Bishop Michael Murphy in an interview with the author, July 1991
2. Seamus Grace in an interview with the author, May 1991
3. Edmund M. Hogan, *The Irish Missionary Movement: A Historical Survey, 1830-1980*, Dublin, Gill & Macmillan, 1990, p 91
4. Fr Michael O'Neill in an interview with the author, July 1991
5. Gerald M. Costello, *Mission to Latin America*, Maryknoll, Orbis Books, 1979, p 44
6. Bishop Michael Murphy, op. cit.
7. *The Far East*, March 1968
8. Fr Michael O'Sullivan SJ in an interview with the author, July 1991
9. Fiodhna Callanan in an interview with the author, June 1991
10. Fr Tom Jordan OP in an interview with the author, July 1991
11. Bishop Michael Murphy, op cit.
12. Bishop Michael Murphy, 'The Parish: The Challenge Ahead', Diocese of Cork, 1986, p 9
13. Bishop Michael Murphy, op. cit.
14. Fr John O'Connell in an interview with the author, July 1991
15. Fr Noel Kerins in an interview with the author, July 1991
16. Fiodhna Callanan, op. cit.
17. Fr Ciaran Earley OMI in an interview with the author, May 1991
18. Fr Michael O'Sullivan SJ, op. cit.
19. Bishop Michael Murphy, op. cit.
20. Fr John O'Connell, op. cit.

Chapter 11

Working for Change: Irish Solidarity with Latin America

"During the 1980s a new element has come into play, arising from the commitment of elements in the otherwise conservative Roman Catholic Church in Ireland (including in particular missionary orders with experience in areas like Central America and the Philippines) to social justice in such countries. This has carried over into a somewhat unconsidered neutralism..."

– Garret FitzGerald TD, Taoiseach, 1981 and 1982-87[1]

Events in Latin America have rarely made an impact on Irish public opinion. It was all the more surprising therefore that in the early 1980s events in El Salvador and Nicaragua, and particularly US policy towards these two countries, touched a nerve end in the Irish psyche and occasioned widespread condemnation of the United States. This culminated in the unprecedented wave of protests which greeted President Reagan when he visited Ireland in June 1984. Three times during the 1980s, Dáil Éireann debated motions on Central America, a virtually unprecedented display of parliamentary interest in a distant region with little or no Irish links. All-party delegations of parliamentarians also visited countries of the region a number of times during the period. These events of the mid-1980s mark a high-point in Irish relations with Latin America and have left their mark on Irish foreign policy.

The roots of this interest may in a general way lie in Irish missionary links with Latin America but it was the founding of Trócaire in 1973 by the Irish Catholic bishops as their agency for world development that was to be the catalyst for developing awareness and action on Central America. In the late 1970s and early 1980s a number of solidarity groups were founded which furthered awareness and practical solidarity with countries of the region. The most notable of these were the Irish El Salvador Support Committee and the Irish Nicaragua Support Group.

The intensive lobbying work of these groups helped to inform and to develop concern among parliamentarians, diplomats and journalists which in turn developed public awareness. By the mid-1980s, the US administration was seriously concerned about the strength of Irish public opinion on Central America and sought to counteract it.

Bringing the issues of development home

A number of decisions made when Trócaire was initially established were to have a long-term effect on the development of Irish awareness about Latin America. Unlike Concern, the other major Irish development agency which concentrates exclusively on Africa and Asia (leaving Latin America to its sister agency in the United States), Trócaire decided to spread its funding evenly over the three continents. Though this has not been possible to sustain in practice, it has meant a far greater percentage of its funds is allocated to Latin America than by any other Irish development agency or by the state. In 1990, Trócaire allocated £912,659 to South America and £263,795 to Central America and the Caribbean out of total allocations of £5.2m.

In supporting such work as leadership training, adult education, human rights promotion and the advancement of women, the programmes on which most of the agency's funds in Latin America are spent, Trócaire puts into practice its desire to support long-term development projects with the full and active participation of the people assisted. Since this work is being done mostly by non-governmental organisations (NGOs), often in the face of active opposition by governments, it is with these that the agency has built close links. Trócaire's director, Brian McKeown, explains that the agency's links with NGOs

> "are much stronger in Latin America than in Africa because the groups in Latin America are much more structured. All our aid goes through NGOs. We don't give any direct assistance to governments in any of these countries. We would hope that the kind of relationship that we have with other NGOs would be one of partnership, not just providing money but trying to understand better the situation which they are working in, their own problems. We also try to give help other than financial assistance. When people have been picked up, we have written to the government involved and made

representations. We have brought to the attention of institutions like the EC exactly what was happening to NGOs on the ground so that the EC in turn could bring pressure to bear on the governments.

So we would see our relationship with them more as a partnership in which they also have a great deal to contribute to us as regards our understanding of the world. We never feel it is a sort of one-way donor-recipient process. We feel we have as much to learn and to gain from working and from being associated with these groups as we have to give them."[2]

This partnership has allowed Trócaire become an active participant in local struggles for justice, an experience which gives it a deeper insight into and involvement in Latin America's problems than might be true of other agencies.

From this involvement with local groups, the agency has become involved in political lobbying at home which Brian McKeown sees

"as part and parcel of our involvement in projects on the ground. In places like El Salvador, we were supporting co-operatives, small agricultural programmes and leadership training and we found that many of the people involved in those projects were being picked up and tortured and we were than asked to provide legal help. So this brought us into the whole area of human rights within El Salvador. It was an automatic follow-through to our commitment to the people in those countries that we got involved in that way. At one stage we were financing Archbishop Romero's radio station which was used to denounce violations of human rights.

Given the situation which we found on the ground in Central America, we felt it was important to try and make Irish politicians more aware of what was happening there so we organised an inter-party delegation to go out there in January 1982. As a result of that we got them to bring pressure on the Irish government to try and influence US foreign policy which we felt was responsible for most of these human rights abuses through the support which the US government was giving the regime in El Salvador."

Another priority Trócaire set early in its existence was the allocation of resources to development education in Ireland, believing that an informed public opinion at home would be in the long-term interests of world development. Brian McKeown says that Trócaire does not "believe that an NGO will ever resolve the problems which exist in the Third World. We don't have the financial resources, we are not multinationals, we are not international banks. So we think it is very important that we try to educate the public here in Ireland, make them aware of the extent and the causes of world poverty and oppression and thus bring pressure on the government. Only governments can solve most of the massive problems and the governments have the financial resources to get the necessary input that we feel is vital."

Encouraging trade unions, solidarity groups

This has led to Trócaire developing links with trade unions and with solidarity groups. Brian McKeown adds:

"We have supported trade union programmes out in the Third World because we feel that it is an important means for people in the Third World to organise themselves in order to get just wages and working conditions. We also feel that it is important to trade unions in the First World countries to participate and be part of that solidarity effort. In fact, we feel it would be more their responsibility than our responsibility. So through our educational programmes, we have tried to raise a level of awareness amongst trade unionists here in Ireland. We produce a bi-monthly bulletin on specific Third World trade union issues which goes to the Irish Congress of Trade Unions and through them to all members of the trade union movement. We have also tried to get some trade unionists out on what we call exposure programmes in the Third World to see the situation of workers for themselves. So when they come back they will start working within their own structures to help create the solidarity links and the support which we feel trade unions need in the Third World."

Brian McKeown says the agency "has not actually been involved with solidarity groups here because we feel Trócaire is not a solidarity group but an institutional agency. What we have tried to do is to encourage the creation of these groups and to give them whatever back-up support we can through information, documentation and things like that. But we feel it is up to them to organise their own activities."

As well as its lobbying work at home, Trócaire has worked to interest the EC in Latin America.

"We have been involved with the EC since we were set up. I was president of the EC Liaison Committee [a committee of representatives of development agencies in EC countries] for a three-year period and we felt as NGOs we had an important political role to play vis-à-vis the EC's policies in the Third World. Because the EC is operating at the level of governments, most of their funds go through the Lomé Convention. When they set up the co-financing system with NGOs, we saw this as a means not just of attaining additional funding; we also saw it as a means of getting the EC to be involved and participate in some of the kinds of projects with some of the kinds of groups which we felt were important to the whole development process and with which normally they wouldn't be involved. These would be groups like human rights groups, co-operatives, even women's groups."

Since the EC had little involvement in Latin America before Spain and Portugal joined in 1986, Trócaire also used the NGO co-financing scheme to interest the Community in Latin America. "We had a deliberate policy of putting projects to them from Latin America rather than projects from Africa so as to help them spread their involvement and their commitment," says Brian McKeown.

Trócaire, through the EC Liaison Committee, has also been involved in more direct lobbying on specific issues. "In relation to the situation in Central America, particularly in El Salvador, we have given testimony before the development committee of the European Parliament in relation to the abuses of human rights in that region," says Brian McKeown. The NGOs have also taken up directly political issues, he points out. "For example, the time that [US Under-Secretary of State, Lawrence] Eagleburger was sent around EC member states to try to convince both the Commission and the member states that they should not be giving aid through non-governmental organisations for refugees and displaced people in Central America, we undertook a big lobby to force the EC not to listen to that message and to carry on giving the aid."

Trócaire is not the only group to carry out such work. The Irish branches of the British agencies Oxfam and Christian Aid support development projects in Latin America and also devote resources to development education and lobbying. Comhlámh, the association of returned development workers, runs its own development education programmes while the Irish Congress of Trade Unions helps raise awareness about development issues among trade unionists through its Third World Committee. The Belfast-based Centre for Research and Documentation (CRD) seeks to develop a Latin American type approach to community issues and to foster grassroots links between Ireland and Latin America. Irish funds are also channelled to projects in Latin America through agencies such as Gorta and Action from Ireland (AFrI), through the Church of Ireland Bishops Appeal and through the Third World funds of a number of trade unions, the civil service, credit unions and companies such as RTÉ and the Bank of Ireland.

Bishop Eamonn Casey's role

While the work of these agencies in developing awareness about Latin America and lobbying for action has often been done quietly with little publicity, the chairman of Trócaire, Bishop Eamonn Casey of Galway, has become an outspoken advocate on behalf of the poor and oppressed in the Third World and notably in Latin America. He attended the funeral of the murdered Archbishop Romero of San Salvador in March 1980 and afterwards was a key eyewitness in refuting Salvadorean government claims that members of the popular organisations had been responsible for the violence outside the cathedral that day. He has since returned to the region on four occasions as a member of Trócaire delegations, visiting El Salvador and Nicaragua in August 1981, Guatemala and Nicaragua in August 1983, Nicaragua, El Salvador and Cuba in November 1985 and El Salvador, Nicaragua and Guatemala in September 1990.

The bishop's vivid first-hand accounts of what he encountered, as well as his outspoken criticism of the policy of the United States administration and its role in the region, has had an impact on public opinion in Ireland. Following his 1981 visit, he called for Ireland to consider breaking off diplomatic relations with the United States if the Reagan administration did not change its Central American policy. He also flew to the United States to brief Archbishop Hickey of Washington, and in particular asked that the US bishops give their support to Archbishop Rivera y Damas of San Salvador. On the same visit, Bishop Casey briefed both the Irish Ambassador to the United Nations, Noel Dorr, and the Irish Foreign Minister, Dr James Dooge, who was in the US to address the UN General Assembly. Another person briefed by Bishop Casey at the time was the Vatican Secretary of State, Cardinal Casaroli.

The bishop's forceful stand was recognised internationally. In June 1985, he was invited by the Argentine Nobel Peace Prize winner and human rights activist, Perez Esquivel, to join a human rights delegation to Peru. The bishop was recommended by Americas Watch and the Washington Office on Latin America (WOLA) which had been impressed by the strong stand he had taken on Central America.

Bishop Casey says that "one of the most important facts in creating awareness has been that we spoke out of the reality that we had experienced ourselves and we spoke with an assurance because the evidence and knowledge we had of the reality were impeccable. These came from two sources: local church groups and Irish Franciscan missionaries working there. No matter what criticisms were made of us in terms of our stand on the issues, any statement we have ever made has never been challenged. We have a policy in Trócaire which I think is very effective. Whenever there is a world focus on some issue, like Archbishop Romero's death, that is the time we go in and educate, educate, educate. We did the same when President Reagan came to visit Ireland."[3]

Solidarity groups: education, lobbying, protesting

The role of solidarity groups in the 1980s in deepening the concern of the Irish public at events in Central America and channelling it in effective ways through lobbying and protest actions was very important. This work began at the time of the Chilean coup in September 1973 when the Irish Committee for Chile was established by left-wing groups. Solidarity work for Chile was, however, hampered by political divisions until the Chile Committee for Human Rights (Ireland) was founded in 1978 under the chairmanship of a Jesuit priest, Fr Kevin Casey. It was later re-named the Ireland-Chile Support Committee in 1984. Meanwhile, some of the twenty-five Chilean families who came to Ireland as political refugees in 1974-75 were also active in raising public awareness about events in Chile. A group of them established a folk group called Mapuché in 1977 which played at venues all around Ireland and issued two music tapes. Despite the consistent work, however, the issue of Chile remained of limited concern and never gained the same prominence in the public mind as did El Salvador and Nicaragua in the 1980s.

The arrest and torture of an Irish priest, Fr Pat Rice, in Buenos Aires in 1976 led to the forming of an Argentine Human Rights Group which for a short period helped to draw attention to the situation in Argentina. With the release of Fr Rice, however, Irish public opinion proved little interested in Argentina and the group remained active for only a short period.

The Irish El Salvador Support Committee was to have a longer life. It grew out of visits home in late 1979 by Irish missionaries working in El Salvador. They were concerned to publicise the repression being experienced by the people among whom they were working and hoped that the Irish government might raise the situation internationally. Through these missionary links, the Committee has access to first-hand information about the true situation in El Salvador which it has used to good effect with politicians and the media. It has also hosted senior opposition spokespersons from El Salvador and organised meetings for them with politicians, journalists and officials of the Department of Foreign Affairs. Though international attention focused little on El Salvador throughout much of the 1980s, the Committee maintained pressure through its network of groups around Ireland for a negotiated settlement and for an end to human rights abuses. As Salvadorean peace negotiations drew to a close in late 1991 and early 1992, the Irish El Salvador Support Committee was again active, drawing attention to the US role in El Salvador and highlighting the need for urgent social and economic reforms if the fundamental cause of the country's problems was to be addressed.

The Irish Nicaragua Support Group (INSG) became by the late 1980s the most organised and active solidarity group on Latin America. It was established following a visit to Ireland by the Nicaraguan Ambassador to Britain, Francisco D'Escoto, in November 1983 and over the following years grew in numbers and extended its activities as events in Nicaragua remained in the public eye. It organised a "Nicaragua Must Survive" campaign, published a Nicaragua Bulletin, organised coffee brigades and study visits to Nicaragua and actively developed support among politicians for Nicaragua. In February 1985, the group facilitated a visit by the vice-president of Nicaragua, Sergio Ramirez, and in May 1989 helped organise a highly publicised visit by President Daniel Ortega, the first visit to Ireland by a Latin American head of state. Though badly shaken by the defeat of the Sandinistas in the February 1990 elections, the INSG has remained in existence seeking to maintain effective solidarity with the people of Nicaragua and to ensure the gains of the revolution are not lost. A weekly protest outside the US Embassy in Dublin was begun following the elections in an attempt to keep public attention on events in Central America. Annual visits to Nicaragua of a group from Ireland continue to be organised by the INSG as do visits to Ireland of prominent figures from Nicaragua and other Central American countries. The Group publishes the *Nica News* three times a year and in early 1992 began a more regular service of information to keep members and other interested people informed about developments in Nicaragua.

A number of smaller solidarity groups have also been active. A Latin American Solidarity Committee, formed in October 1980, devoted much of its attention to Guatemala and mounted exhibitions on human rights abuses there. Out of it were born the INSG and a Peru Support Group. The latter was formed in November 1984 to highlight human rights abuses in Peru but remained inactive for a number of years before being re-formed in 1990 as the situation in Peru worsened considerably. It publishes the quarterly bulletin *Peru Today* and has mounted an exhibition in Dublin to raise awareness about Peru. A Guatemala Information Group is also active publishing a bulletin called *Guatemala News*. Action from Ireland (AFrI), an NGO which seeks to link issues of injustice in the Third World with such issues in Ireland, played a prominent role in organising the protests during the Reagan visit in 1984. In 1986, it helped establish a Church Group in Solidarity with Nicaragua after the Nicaraguan Foreign Minister, Fr Miguel D'Escoto, appealed during a visit to Ireland for Irish Church people to respond to the plight of Nicaragua. A focal point of activity for many of these groups is Central America Week which is held every March. An Irish Brazil Solidarity Group was formed in 1991 with, among its aims, that of helping Irish people to learn from the Brazilian experience of community development, adult education and church organisation. The Ireland-Cuba Friendship Society is the only friendship society in Ireland with any Latin American country. Established in 1978, it has helped sponsor cultural and sporting links between the two countries and in 1988 helped organise an official delegation of Cuban parliamentarians on an official visit to the Oireachtas. In late 1991 a Cuban Solidarity Campaign was established to highlight the plight of Cuba, to campaign for the ending of the US blockade and to raise money to send medical supplies to the island. (Appendix III lists these solidarity groups.)

The Reagan visit

President Ronald Reagan's visit to Ireland from 1-4 June 1984 became a focal point for expression of the strong public disquiet felt in Ireland at aspects of US foreign policy, particularly its Central American policy. Media coverage of the visit was dominated for weeks before the presidential party arrived by criticism of US policies by different groups, with clergy featuring prominently. An opinion poll in *The Irish Times* showed a majority of Irish people would prefer someone else to be US president and during the visit far more people turned out to participate in protests than greeted the president and his wife. So worried was the White House about the rising wave of protests that President Reagan granted RTÉ's "Today Tonight" programme a rare television interview before the visit. During the interview, he argued that his Central American critics were the victims of a Cuban-Soviet misinformation campaign; in reply Trócaire detailed over twenty factual errors made by the president in his references to the region. Bishop Casey charged that it was the US administration which was guilty of spreading misinformation.

Of particular embarrassment to the White House was the effective boycott of the visit by the Irish Catholic bishops. An auxiliary bishop of Dublin was the only bishop to attend a function at which President Reagan was present while Cardinal Ó Fiaich let it be known that he was glad to have an engagement outside the country at the time and Bishop Casey said he was not going to meet the president in order to show solidarity with the oppressed people of the Third World.

Hundreds of priests and sisters participated in protests against Mr Reagan. Saying that "fasting exorcises evil spirits," a group of seventy priests and sisters fasted outside the Garden of Remembrance in Dublin from the moment the president's plane touched down on Irish soil until the moment he left. Clergy and religious also led the protest of some 10,000 people that circled Dublin Castle while President Reagan attended a state banquet within. Four sisters carried a coffin and four bouquets of flowers, each of which bore the name of one of the four US church women killed in El Salvador in 1980. On the mountains overlooking the village of Ballyporeen, from where Mr Reagan's great grandfather was supposed to have emigrated in 1849, a huge white cross was laid out in memory of Archbishop Romero. When, during the short prayer service in the village church attended by President and Mrs Reagan, a priest prayed for the victims of repression throughout the world, a quiet handclap rippled through the congregation.

The decision of the National University of Ireland to award the president an honorary degree of law led to unprecedented opposition from the university staff and graduates who focused particularly on Mr Reagan's refusal to recognise the verdict of the International Court of Justice on the mining of Nicaraguan harbours by the United States. At a ceremony held just hours before the president was honoured, three holders of honorary degrees returned their degrees to the university. Many members of the academic staff refused to attend the conferring and on the day before two academics sold photocopies of honorary degrees on the streets of Galway for 10p saying that they would be worthless the following day. In Dublin, a peace camp set up by thirty-three women, including one nun, outside the US Ambassador's residence in the Phoenix Park where President Reagan spent his final night in Ireland, was broken up by the Gardaí, the women illegally detained for over thirty hours and refused their legal rights. A young man who waved a Nicaraguan flag at the president's car as it passed was physically manhandled by Gardaí and two companions were arrested for unfurling posters. As Manuel Bravo, the representative in Ireland of the Salvadorean FDR-FMLN opposition summed up the visit: "This weekend the Irish experienced a little of what Latin Americans have been experiencing for decades."[4]

Perhaps the most notable protest, however, took place in Leinster House when President Reagan addressed a joint session of the Dáil and Seanad. Over twenty members stayed away in protest while three voiced their criticisms and then left the chamber before Mr Reagan rose to speak. The government also distanced itself from US policy on Central America when the Taoiseach, Dr Garret FitzGerald, told the president he favoured talks between the Salvadorean government and the guerrillas and when, during the Dublin Castle banquet, he expressed the hope that relations between Washington and Managua might be normalised. Both positions were vehemently opposed by the US administration at the time.

Influencing the decision-makers

While the extent of activity which developed through the 1980s on issues related to Latin America is impressive, its impact on the Irish foreign policy establishment was probably its greatest achievement. In general, Irish politicians have traditionally paid little attention to issues of foreign policy and this inattention is more marked the further the issues are from our shores. The Fine Gael MEP for Dublin, Mary Banotti, contrasts Ireland with other EC countries in this regard. Elsewhere, she says, there is a much higher level of interest among elected representatives in foreign policy but a much lower level of interest among the general public than in Ireland.[5]

This lack of political interest in foreign affairs is reflected in the lack of structures for debating foreign affairs within most Irish political parties. The Fine Gael TD, Nora Owen, recalls that when her party was in government from 1982-87, it had no forum for developing policy even on sensitive issues like Nicaragua. Deputy Owen, who chaired the Oireachtas Committee on Development Cooperation, said at the time that without the activities of outside development agencies and solidarity groups (NGOs) "even the minimal amount of discussion that goes on would not take place. I think you could count on four hands the number of the 166 Dáil members who would be interested in wider foreign policy issues".[6] The situation has improved slightly since then, she says, with more TDs showing an interest in foreign affairs. The Fine Gael parliamentary party in early 1991 established a number of committees, among them a general affairs committee which has held a number of debates on foreign affairs. Young Fine Gael also has an active foreign affairs committee, Deputy Owen points out.

Unlike the larger parties, Labour has an international committee and an international secretary. It is also active in the Socialist International (SI) which it joined in 1968. Like other SI members, the party took a keen interest in the Socialist Unity government of Salvador Allende in Chile and played a role in maintaining SI links with Chilean parties following the 1973 coup. Tony Brown, the party's international secretary, says: "It is very hard to translate the level of interest and debate on issues like Central America that one encounters in the Socialist International back into the Irish system."[7] The Workers Party has also taken a greater interest in Latin America and maintains links with a number of socialist parties in the region. The former party leader, Proinsias de Rossa, said the party saw Latin America "as a sort of cockpit of the struggle between the small person and this overwhelming American imperialism, trying to dominate parts of the world. So from a political point of view it is important for us to demonstrate solidarity with people who are struggling against that kind of odds."[8] The Labour Party is the only Irish party with a stated policy on Latin America while the Workers Party mentions Latin America in its policy document on development aid.

In the absence of an Oireachtas foreign affairs committee, formulation of foreign policy is left to officials of the Department of Foreign Affairs. Nora Owen thinks some of these officials fear a foreign affairs committee could become a forum for anti-US sentiment. As a TD of the party in government from 1982 to 1987, she remembers that the best way she could influence policy was to go directly to the Minister for Foreign Affairs. "I felt that the Department's line on these issues [such as Latin America] remained very much the line of the Minister. There was never any real discussion about changing policy and I felt there was an inordinate attempt to ensure you didn't embarrass....I do feel there is a pro-US line. I am not saying there should not be – there are a number of things I would support the US on – but I feel that there is a little too much conservatism in the Department on a number of these issues."

Another TD who has taken an active interest in Latin America since his student days is Michael D. Higgins of Labour. He believes Irish policy "is crucially influenced by the high level of dependency on multinational investment in the Irish economy." He said he has no doubt that "Central and Latin American issues were put into the freezer by the United States participation in the Anglo-Irish Agreement [signed in 1985]. I remember being requested very definitely by people (whom I will not name) to go easy on these issues while the Anglo-Irish Agreement was going on. I thought it was outrageous."[9]

When the NGOs began a serious attempt to influence Irish policy on Latin America in the early 1980s therefore they entered a situation completely unused to such lobbying. The Labour Party's international secretary, Tony Brown, believes that the NGOs "have been extremely effective." They have resources to devote to raising awareness on issues like Latin America that the political parties do not have, he said, and he notices that "when the NGOs are really showing interest in an issue you get an upsurge in interest among the politicians." One of the most effective means of getting parliamentarians to take an interest in Latin American issues has been through all-party delegations to different countries of the region. This was begun by Trócaire which organised all-party delegations to El Salvador and Nicaragua in 1982. This was followed by delegations to monitor the Nicaraguan elections in 1984 and again in 1990, a delegation to Nicaragua and Cuba in 1986 and delegations to monitor the plebiscite in Chile in 1988 and the subsequent elections in 1989. On all occasions, the main parties in Dáil Éireann were represented thus ensuring that on return Latin American issues were raised within each of them. As a result of this, for example, a group of around six Fianna Fáil TDs established an ad hoc group to discuss Latin American issues, made up mostly of members who had visited the region on various delegations. Niall Andrews, now an MEP, was on the first such delegation and has remained active on Latin American issues since. As a result, he said, "the party has in general taken on a supportive role in Latin America which is a very big change from ten years ago when they wouldn't have known where El Salvador or Nicaragua were. Things have changed considerably."[10] Niall Andrews acknowledges the major role Trócaire played in this change.

As a result of this interest, three all-party motions have been passed in the Dáil on Central America and questions have been regularly raised on Latin American issues. The Foreign Minister during the period when interest was most alive on Central America was Peter Barry and he remembers the "tremendous interest in Ireland in Nicaragua and what was going on there. This was broadening our knowledge because questions were being tabled in the Dáil regularly to which I had to respond. So that helped us [in formulating our policy]. I think you must thank Trócaire a lot for that interest." In the absence of Irish embassies in the region which could provide first-hand information, he sought to set up a channel of information on Central America through the Socialist International. "It was obviously very good and was balancing the kind of information I was getting from my sources in America and Europe. I was anxious to have it," he said.[11]

The results were visible in policy declarations at the time. As early as September 1981, Senator James Dooge who was then Foreign Minister mentioned El Salvador in his address to the General Assembly of the UN saying the situation there "is a matter of particular concern to many people in Ireland." He went on to say that "Ireland accepts the principles underlying the recent [August 1981] Franco-Mexican Declaration" [recognising the FDR-FMLN as a representative political force]. Though falling short of giving complete support to that controversial declaration, Ireland's position was at the time considered positive by lobbyists and NGOs at home and reflected the extent to which their pressure had had an impact. On Nicaragua also, Ireland has taken a stand generally supportive of the Sandinistas. Michael D. Higgins thinks that "no Irish diplomat would feel free to take anything other than a progressive line in relation to Nicaragua because of public opinion." Gerard Collins, Foreign Minister to 1992 agrees that "the public interest which was expressed here obviously contributed to a greater focus on Central America and its problems both at national level and in political co-operation with our EC partners."[12] Yet not all agree. Many active on Central American issues believe Ireland is not forceful enough in putting its point of view forward in the EC and the UN. Niall Andrews said he "would like to see Ireland take a more positive role on the whole Central America issue."

Countering the NGOs

If NGO activity had an impact on Irish policy during the 1980s, it was obvious that not all in the foreign policy establishment welcomed this new influence though antipathy or even opposition was rarely articulated publicly. A speech by a former Irish Ambassador to Washington and former Secretary of the Department of Foreign Affairs, Sean Donlon, to the Ireland-United States Chamber of Commerce in November 1989 was all the more revealing therefore in that it publicly stated a position that must broadly represent that of a certain sector of Irish foreign policy makers (see Appendix II). Referring to the traditionally close relationship between Ireland and the United States, Sean Donlon quoted from an article in *The Los Angeles Times* which lamented the anti-Americanism of Irish foreign policy. He could not say this represented "an incomplete or somewhat unbalanced analysis of Irish foreign policy", he said, though he would like to think it did and he pointed to such evidence for the article's assertion as the protests against President Reagan during his visit to Ireland and in general "the number of protests outside the US Embassy in Dublin" which "has long since overtaken those outside the British Embassy." He also pointed to Ireland's stance at the UN which, he said, "is more often out of line with the Western consensus than most other EC member countries." In seeking to lay blame for these developments, of which he obviously does not approve, Sean Donlon lamented that "a tendency has emerged which encourages small interest groups to dominate the debate and to set an agenda for the conduct of the Irish-American relationship which is essentially dominated by a spirit of anti-Americanism." As proponents of this "tendency" he singled out "Roman Catholic clerical [voices] whose utterances still tend to have a megaphonic effect". What is most notable about the controversial assertions in this speech is that they acknowledge the impact of the NGO lobby on Irish foreign policy during this period was greater than that of Mr Donlon, then the chief civil servant with responsibility for foreign policy. The speech also signals a certain flexing of muscles by those who want a rather more tame and predictable foreign policy.

Garret FitzGerald, Taoiseach during the period of most active Irish interest in Latin America, appears to share some of Mr Donlon's antipathy towards the NGO lobby on foreign policy. In an article on Irish neutrality in the summer 1987 issue of a magazine published in Amsterdam, *European Affairs*, Dr FitzGerald wrote about groups who saw Ireland's traditional neutrality as being under threat. "During the 1980s a new element has come into play, arising from the commitment of elements in the otherwise conservative Roman Catholic Church in Ireland (including in particular missionary orders with experience in areas like Central America and the Philippines) to social justice in such countries. This has carried over into a somewhat unconsidered neutralism, which led the Conference of Major Religious Superiors prior to the referendum on the Single European Act to issue a statement which suggested that in some way Irish neutrality is a *moral* issue as distinct from one of policy and of reflecting the present wishes of the Irish electorate – a statement which I challenged in the Dáil during the debate on the Single European Act referendum proposal."[13] In the next paragraph of his article, however, Dr FitzGerald appears to acknowledge that the NGO lobby he criticises reflects public opinion on the issue of neutrality better than do the main political parties. Referring to opinion polls which show that about 85 per cent of the public favour the maintaining of military neutrality, Dr FitzGerald writes that "the political parties, sensitive to the strength of public opinion, have not been disposed to challenge popular sentiment, and the two principal parties have indeed to some extent moved back from the position they adopted during the 1972 referendum campaign, of openness towards an eventual European defence arrangement in the context of an eventual European confederation or federation."

Since the mid-1980s, the impact of the NGO lobby has been counteracted by a number of factors. Among these is the growing co-ordination of foreign policy through European political co-operation (EPC). Peter Barry admits that "more and more we are being influenced by trying to find a position with the other twelve member states as regards our foreign policy."[14] Sally O'Neill of Trócaire also sees a change in the attitude of the Department of Foreign Affairs to NGOs: "I think that the situation in the last few years has changed substantially and there is a tremendous resentment of anybody who wants to make statements. I see a clear rejection of NGOs. The informal relationships that allowed access to them, to discuss things with them, seems to have gone now. I think the Americans definitely played a role there."[15]

Others also identify the influence of the US embassy which stepped up its lobbying to try to counteract that of the NGO lobby. Michael D. Higgins recalls that when Peter Dailey took up his appointment as US Ambassador to Ireland in 1982 "he was very, very upset at the degree of knowledge and opposition that existed to US activity in Central America." As well as being Ambassador to Ireland, he had a special responsibility for pushing the US line on Central America with governments throughout the EC. Senior State Department officials were brought to Dublin to brief politicians and other public figures and regular documents were sent to them to counteract the facts and opinions put forward in documents produced by Trócaire and solidarity groups. At the time of the April 1983 all-party motion in the Dáil, US officials were reported to have made efforts to change the wording of the motion. These efforts backfired when they became the object of angry exchanges on the floor of the House.

Bishop Casey also recalls numerous invitations to him to meet visiting US officials on Central America. He waited until he had two US Catholic Church officials visiting Ireland to take them to the US Embassy to show that similar opposition to US policies existed in the United States and that such opposition in no way indicated anti-American sentiment on his part. According to Michael D. Higgins, one of the ways direct pressure was brought to bear on politicians was through the US Chamber of Commerce in Ireland. They would contact US multinationals in the constituencies of deputies who were supportive of the interparty motions in the Dáil. "Those deputies in constituencies with large US multinationals would therefore get uncomfortable about supporting our motions," said Michael D. Higgins.

Footnotes

1. Garret FitzGerald TD, 'Irish Neutrality', in *European Affairs*, No 2, summer 1987, p 27
2. Brian McKeown in an interview with the author, March 1988
3. Bishop Eamonn Casey in an interview with the author, March 1988
4. 'Irish Protest Focuses on Central America', in *Latinamerica Press*, 5 July 1984, pp 3,4
5. Mary Banotti MEP in an interview with the author, March 1988
6. Nora Owen TD in an interview with the author, March 1988
7. Tony Brown in an interview with the author, March 1988
8. Proinsias de Rossa TD in an interview with the author, March 1988

9. Michael D. Higgins TD in an interview with the author, March 1988
10. Niall Andrews MEP in an interview with the author, March 1988
11. Peter Barry TD in an interview with the author, March 1988
12. Gerard Collins TD in written answers to questions supplied by the author, August 1991
13. Garret FitzGerald TD, op. cit.
14. Peter Barry TD, op. cit.
15. Sally O'Neill in an interview with the author, March 1988

Chapter 12

Future Links: Ireland and Latin America in the 1990s

"I think it is possible to work with some of my ideas in Ireland. I am sure it is...It is a question of knowing – how to challenge the oppressed people of Ireland to know, to read their reality?"

– Paulo Freire, Brazilian educationalist[1]

Ireland and Latin America enter the 1990s in a state of major transition with the future full of uncertainty. As a member of the European Community, Ireland is pooling its sovereignty to an ever greater degree and, though giving the deepening integration a general welcome, is fearful that growth in the core countries will take place at the expense of the periphery. Latin America too is beginning on a similar road with certain fears that deepening integration with the United States may imperil its weak industrial and services sector thus leaving it further marginalised. Yet, as countries with weak peripheral economies, neither Ireland nor Latin America see any alternative. There is much to play for.

However, certain Latin American countries seem to recognise better the potential for developing bilateral economic links than does Ireland. Mexico has gone so far as to open an embassy in Dublin, a move not reciprocated by Ireland. Chile has also made overtures to establish diplomatic links and closer trading relations which have been cooly received. Significantly the Chileans cited our historical links in the person of Bernardo O'Higgins as one of the reasons; such concerns seem to matter little to the Irish side. If one of the main reasons both Mexico and Chile are interested in developing links with Ireland is to gain a foothold in the EC to avail of the benefits of full integration after 1992, similar reasons could interest us in such links as both countries are negotiating free trade treaties with the United States.

Our reluctance to respond to such overtures accurately reflects our neglect of the Latin American region both as a market and as a part of the world with which we could develop a fruitful political dialogue on a bilateral level from which both sides would have a lot to learn. Indeed as our foreign policy is formulated more and more in the context of European Political Co-operation (EPC), the need to complement EC links with distinctively Irish links seems to be forgotten. Our relatively good record in championing Latin American concerns within EPC should not be a substitute for an Irish voice where necessary. It is difficult to disagree with those who argue that if Ireland were called upon today to take the same stand on El Salvador or Nicaragua as it did in the early and mid 1980s, Ireland would be far more reluctant to do so.

Ireland's neglect of bilateral links with Latin America indicates the narrow horizons of our foreign policy. Underlying this is the lack of resources which do not allow the development of a more adequate network of embassies and thereby a greater pool of specialist knowledge within our foreign service. Yet the failure to fund a more adequate foreign service may be a foolhardy economy as a more forceful projection of ourselves on the world stage should open greater trading opportunities. The lack of resources seems to mirror a lack of will to develop an independent presence, a refusal to face the valuable experience we have to offer as a former colony seeking to develop economically and socially and the need to learn from others in a similar situation.

An example of an issue where we have valuable experience to offer which could benefit from active consideration is the long-term legacy of colonialism as an impediment to economic and social development. The Irish state seems unaware of the need to pursue such issues or to develop wider links with the post-colonial world. This suggests we are unwilling to address the structural causes of our underdevelopment, especially in regard to unemployment.

In the absence of official efforts, it has been left to private bodies to develop these links. The impact of Latin American concerns on the consciousness of sectors of the Irish public in the 1980s shows the potential for closer links. The few Irish academics who teach courses on Latin America such as Dr Ciaran Cosgrove of the Spanish Department, Trinity College, Dublin, and Dr Dermot Keogh of the Modern History Department in University College, Cork, testify to the interest in Latin America that exists among the student body. The growing numbers of Irish missionaries who choose Latin America as a place to work is further evidence that contemporary Irish people find in Latin America a place which invigorates them and where there is much to learn. They too have shown themselves aware that Ireland could benefit from closer links with Latin America.

It is then at this unofficial level that most prospects for closer links with Latin America exist. There is every reason to believe that solidarity groups will continue to raise public awareness about countries like El Salvador, Guatemala, Nicaragua, Peru, Brazil and Chile. Another group established in 1990 which reflects Latin American concerns is the Irish Network on Debt and Development, affiliated to the European network. These groups may rarely make headlines but their work is developing awareness both among the general public and among politicians and is generating new perspectives from which Irish people have much to learn.

Missionary links also look set to grow and flourish. As the Irish Catholic Church faces the challenge of adapting to a pluralist society and of discovering for itself a role in the Ireland of tomorrow, the experience of Latin America will have much to offer. In particular the new understanding of Church-state relations in which the Church sees itself as a voice for the voiceless and the new model of "people's church" through which lay people, and especially the poor, win for themselves a key place in Church life, have much to offer the Irish Church if it is not to become more irrelevant in the years ahead. In this context the attempts of returned missionaries to feed back their experiences in effective ways take on added importance.

Ultimately, however, there is probably one thing more than any other that Ireland urgently needs to learn from Latin America and to which the quote from Paulo Freire at the beginning of this chapter refers. This is the Latin American ability to do a serious reading of the *coyuntura*, as they call it, drawing out the different political, economic, social, cultural and ecclesiastical strands that go to make up the national or international situation at any given moment of time. Such a reading which seeks to comprehend the political, cultural and social factors as well as the merely economic in any understanding of the forces at work in shaping a society, provides a far fuller basis for elaborating future policies and plans than does the rather narrow readings which are the norm in Ireland. If we could learn from Latin America the ability to do such a reading of the Irish story, particularly of the changes we have experienced over the past thirty years, we could perhaps discover a way of breaking out of the pervasive sense of despair and paralysis that grips so many people in Ireland who rightly reject the false sense of optimism generated by our political and business elites. And in such a reading we might discover what is Latin America's greatest gift to the world, its irrepressible sense of hope that things can be better not just for the elites but for the poor majority. If we could learn something of that hope we would have a potent resource for building a better Ireland.

Footnote
1. Paulo Freire in an interview with the author, published in *The Irish Times*, 21 January 1981

Appendix I

Extracts from a speech by the former Irish Ambassador to the UN, Noel Dorr, to the UN General Assembly on 29 November 1982 on a resolution to declare 1992 the year of the fifth centennial of the discovery of America.

The draft resolution before us would have the General Assembly declare 1992 the year of the fifth centennial of the discovery of America. It would ask the Secretary-General to prepare the appropriate observances to commemorate this great event and it would request him to submit an annual report on the progress achieved.

The draft resolution, like the original request to inscribe the item on the agenda has wide sponsorship. The list includes many countries from Latin America and the Caribbean, the countries of North America and some countries among those in Western Europe with a history of seafaring and exploration.

No one could wish to deny the historic importance of the voyage of Columbus, or the fact that it was indeed, as the draft resolution says, "a decisive step towards the achievement of a clear conception of our planet." We certainly would not wish to deny the "contribution by the peoples of the New World to progress and understanding among nations", and any draft resolution which has such a wide and disparate sponsorship and which brings together certain countries from North America and the Caribbean which are otherwise hostile to each other should be given the most careful consideration.

Nevertheless, despite our good will towards all of the countries which have sponsored it, we have some doubts about the wisdom of the adoption by the Assembly of the present draft resolution. The draft proposed the commemoration of 12 October 1992 as the 500th anniversary of the discovery of America. It is true that the landing by Columbus on the island of San Salvador on 12 October 1492 was an important event, but is it not something of an exaggeration to speak so confidently of it as "the discovery of America"? For one thing, there were already at that time indigenous inhabitants in America, North and South. They had lived here for many thousands of years; they had diverse and highly developed cultures of their own – some of which had waxed and waned well before the arrival of Columbus; and their descendants today might well have their own very particular view of the significance for their peoples of that historic event.

Furthermore, even if one speaks of the first European contacts with the Americas it is by no means clear that the record begins only in 1492. There is reasonably good evidence that the Norsemen, and in particular Leif Ericsson, discovered the New World about the year 1000 and established some settlements in North America.

I am reluctant to appear in any way nationalistic or chauvinistic in speaking of such a matter, but I cannot refrain from mentioning also Irish stories and legends which received wide currency in Europe in the Middle Ages in the Latin text known as *Navigatio Sancti Brendani*, which suggest that Irish monks may have made the dangerous crossing of the North Atlantic as early as the seventh century. This has been referred to already by Ambassador Albornoz of Ecuador with his customary generosity. It is perhaps not clearly established whether St Brendan the Navigator, the Irish monk in question, was a historic figure or whether he did in fact complete such a voyage as the medieval text credits him with – though I would not like to dispute the fact in County Kerry where he is the local patron saint. Within the past few years a modern adventurer has built and sailed a similar boat from Ireland to North America along the route which St Brendan might have taken and has thus proved the voyage to be at least possible.

Perhaps to avoid appearing too nationalistic I might quote from an eminent and detached historian. The historian is Samuel Eliot Morison, who wrote as follows on page 18 of his monumental work *The Oxford History of the American People*:

> "Norsemen discovered the New World about the year 1000 and an unknown Irishman probably did so even earlier.
>
> "It is a historical fact that Irishmen discovered and settled Iceland when it was empty of human life, and that Norsemen expelled them about AD 850. The same sagas which describe the Norse discoveries call certain lands west of Greenland 'white man's land' or 'Ireland the Great' and add a few interesting details."

I must admit that on the following page Morison detracts a little from the assurance of that quotation when he says the following:

> "Some day perchance authentic Irish relics will be found in north eastern Canada but until that time comes we have only

these elusive stories of an Irish colony glimpsed vaguely through the Northern mists."

To say all of this – to mention the earlier indigenous inhabitants, the legends of Irish monks and the more solidly attested evidence of Viking discoveries – is not in any way to grudge or lessen the importance of the landing by Columbus in 1492. For one thing there is another story – apocryphal, no doubt – that Columbus actually stopped on the way in Ireland to pray in the Church of St Nicholas in Galway. More seriously, however, the historic links in recent centuries of Ireland and Irish immigrants with all of the countries of the New World – of North and South America and the Caribbean – have been particularly close, and I recognise that. I do feel, however, as the Assembly is about to adopt a decision in triumphal terms calling for the commemoration ten years hence of the voyage of Columbus, that the points I made earlier should at least be mentioned before we proceed to vote.

Beyond this, and allowing for the understandable desire of the countries of the Americas and other great countries such as Spain, Portugal, Italy and the Philippines, to celebrate Columbus' epic voyage, I wonder if it is necessary for the Assembly to act ten years in advance of the date of the proposed commemoration? In particular, is it wise or necessary for us to ask the Secretary General to submit to the General Assembly over each of the next ten years an annual report on the progress achieved in preparation for this commemoration? In the case of other draft resolutions requesting the Secretary-General to undertake new activities, amendments have been put forward by some delegations requiring that the new activity be limited to what can be done within the limits of the existing two-year programme budget. I would naturally hesitate to put forward such an amendment to the present draft resolution; but I do think it is not a wise idea to ask the Secretary-General to report each year for ten successive years on preparations for a commemoration – however important it may be to many delegations – to be held in 1992.

In conclusion, I must emphasise again that my delegation does not deny the historic importance of Columbus' voyage to the New World; nor, as the draft resolution says, "the...role played by the Spanish nation and Crown in this discovery", nor, as it also says, the growing contribution by the peoples of the New World to progress and understanding among nations. We recognise and acknowledge all these things but we felt that before the Assembly adopts the present draft resolution it should be reminded, however briefly, that the New World was already inhabited at that stage and that other voyagers from Europe had probably reached there by then, even if they made little of their discovery...

Views such as those voiced by the Irish ambassador obviously annoyed the representatives of some of those countries sponsoring the resolution. This was expressed by interventions by the Spanish and certain Latin American Ambassadors later on the same day. The Guatemalan Ambassador lamented "the mockery offered here on certain aspects of the matter." Following him, Mr Dorr made a brief intervention:

In order to avoid any misunderstanding, I should like to emphasise, as indeed I tried to do in my statement, that I had no intention of causing any offence to the countries which sponsored the draft resolution or to detract in any way from the importance of the voyage of Columbus or, indeed, the desirability of commemorating his voyage suitably. Ireland has too high a regard for Spain itself, for Latin America and for the countries of the Hispanic tradition generally to do that. I would therefore emphasise my sincere hope that nothing I said in a light-hearted way in referring to earlier voyages or legends be taken as offensive by the sponsors of the draft resolution."

A decision on the resolution was deferred for a year.

Appendix II

Speech by former Irish Ambassador to the US and Secretary of the Department of Foreign Affairs Sean Donlon to the Ireland-United States Chamber of Commerce, 21 November 1989

Looked at from this side of the Atlantic, we have no difficulty in working on the assumption that the United States is a staunch friend and can be relied on for support and help whenever we need it. Historically, we have done well by the Irish-American relationship and in recent years we have come almost to take for granted the close political relationship that exists between Dublin and Washington and the benefits that flow from it.

To give but a few examples: Ireland continues to benefit not only from US investment, tourism and fund-raising for Irish charities but from the vital support in the negotiation of the 1985 Anglo-Irish Agreement and the generous support given to that Agreement by the United States through the International Fund for Ireland. Washington has to date committed over US$100 million to that Fund, a very significant gesture at a time of public expenditure cutbacks in the US and increasing demands on the US purse from other countries, most recently those in eastern Europe.

Another benefit from the good political relationship between Dublin and Washington has been the major aviation rights conceded to Aer Lingus recently which will enable them to introduce a new service next year into Los Angeles.

In recent years we have also seen a generous response to the renewed Irish emigration wave. In response to Irish lobbying, special arrangements, mainly the Donnelly visas, have been introduced under which twenty thousand Irish people have been or will be enabled to settle permanently in the US. No country has fared better in the re-allocation of visas than Ireland.

So we sit here smugly in Ireland and take it for granted that all is well. We love America. They love us and, from time to time, they give us generous gifts because they love us and because our fellow countrymen and women in years gone by helped to make the US what it is today.

May I invite you now to look at the Irish-American relationship from another angle – that of a hard-nosed politician or administrator in Washington or of an informed US foreign policy analyst. It would be unfair to refer in public to remarks made in private by Washington politicians and administrators. It is possible to refer to a major article which reflects those views and which appeared recently in the *Los Angeles Times*. It was also incidentally, syndicated in the *International Herald Tribune*. The article was written by the respected foreign policy commentator, William Pfaff. Let me give you the flavour of the article by quoting some extracts.

> *"the Irish political class doesn't much like the United States of recent yearss;*
> *"the Irish anti-Americanism is not just an elite phenomenon;*
> *"it is an anti-Americanism led by the Catholic clergy;*
> *"anti-Americanism and foreign policy debate itself is cost-free in Ireland".*

The overall tone of the article is that Ireland's foreign policy is fundamentally anti-American and that its EC policy is neutralist. There is a clear implication that being a part of the West or espousing Western values are not matters of much importance to us. I would like to think that the article reflects an incomplete or somewhat unbalanced analysis of Irish foreign policy. But I am not so sure. Let me give you some "for instances".

1. When have you last heard a speech by an Irish political leader stressing our membership of the family of Western states and our adherence to western values? When we joined the United Nations in 1955, Liam Cosgrave as Minister for External Affairs indicated Ireland's intention "to avoid becoming associated with particular blocks of groups as far as possible" but was emphatic that "we belong to the great community of states made up of the US, Canada and Western Europe". Sean Lemass in the sixties and Jack Lynch and again Liam Cosgrave in the seventies repeated that position. We haven't heard much about it in the last decade.

2. When President Kennedy visited Ireland in 1963 senior representatives of the Catholic Church were everywhere in evidence. When President Reagan visited in 1985, they were conspicuous by their absence.

3. When President Kennedy visited Ireland, the universities fell over themselves to offer him honorary degrees. When President Reagan visited Ireland there was controversy when the National University of Ireland conferred an honorary doctorate on him at University College, Galway.

4. The number of protests outside the US Embassy in Dublin has long since overtaken those outside the British Embassy.

5. When votes are taken on foreign policy issues at the UN, Ireland is more often out of line with the western consensus than most other EC member countries.

The *Los Angeles Times* article will have been worthwhile if it

makes us sit up and pay careful attention to what can happen when some voices, including Roman Catholic clerical ones whose utterances still tend to have a megaphonic effect, are allowed dominate the articulation of the Irish-American relationship. We are *in* the West, we are *of* the West, and that is where our present and future interests lie. No volume of shouting or picketing will change that.

As a sovereign independent country we have a right, even a duty, to establish our own foreign policy agenda. An Irish agenda is unlikely to coincide in all respects with that of the US and there may even be sharp differences on specific issues. It is entirely right that when our interests do differ, we should not attempt to conceal the difference or be afraid to pay an economic price for a principled political position. But a tendency has emerged which encourages small interest groups to dominate the debate and to set an agenda for the conduct of the Irish-American relationship which is essentially dominated by a spirit of anti-Americanism. The main point I wish to make today is that that is wrong in itself and likely to damage rather than promote the real interests of Ireland.

Our interests will continue to be served by politically anchoring ourselves firmly in the West and working in close co-operation with those who are also anchored there.

In the first half of next year, we will have a unique opportunity to contribute to the achievement of Western interests through our Presidency of the European Communities. One of the major political questions facing the Taoiseach and his colleagues in Government in that six month period will be the conduct of relations between the West and the rapidly changing countries of the East. The European Community has been given the lead role in conducting the dialogue between the West on the one hand and Poland and Hungary on the other. These are countries with which we are particularly well placed to liaise because of the many shared religious and historical experiences. But the Irish voice will be an authentic and strong one on this as on other issues only if it is situated in the context of a foreign policy which shamelessly asserts our commitment to Western values and acknowledges the benefits we have derived from the close relationship that exists between us and countries such as the US.

It is appropriate in this week of Thanksgiving and at this meeting of the Ireland-US Chamber of Commerce that an Irish message of thanks should be heard by our American friends. You have been good friends and we will continue to work hard to maintain that friendship.

Appendix III

Solidarity groups involved in work for Latin America

Cuban Solidarity Campaign
17 Hillcrest View, Lucan, Co. Dublin

El Salvador Awareness
St. Clare's Convent, Romero Room,
101 Harold's Cross Road, Dublin 6W

Guatemala Information Group
61 Lower Camden Street, Dublin 2

Honduras Rights Project
61 Lower Camden Street, Dublin 2

Ireland-Chile Support Committee
c/o St. Francis Xavier Church,
Gardiner Street, Dublin 1

Irish Brazil Solidarity Group
St. Clare's Convent, Romero Room,
101 Harold's Cross Road, Dublin 6W.

Irish El Salvador Support Committee
Pennock Hill, Swords, Co. Dublin

Irish Nicaragua Support Group
61 Lower Camden Street, Dublin 2

Peru Support Group
All Hallows College, Grace Park Road,
Drumcondra, Dublin 9

Details of NGOs involved with Latin America are available from:
Congood
59 Deerpark Road
Mount Merrion
Co. Dublin

Bibliography

Part One:
An Irish Reading of the Latin American Story

I consulted a number of the general histories of Latin America in writing this section. Foremost among these are *A Short History of Latin America* by Benjamin Keen and Mark Wasserman (Houghton Mifflin Company, Boston, 1980), which despite its title is a substantial work of 527 pages, and *Modern Latin America* by Thomas E. Skidmore and Peter H. Smith (Oxford University Press, second edition 1989). *Faces of Latin America* by Duncan Green (LAB, London, 1991) is an excellent and up-to-date thematic introduction to Latin America which proved a useful reference work. *The Penguin History of Latin America* by Edwin Williamson (Allen Lane, London, 1992) was published as I was completing this book but still provided some useful final reading, particularly on the economic policies of current Latin American governments.

I have also found the works of Eduardo Galeano very useful in providing a stimulating and challenging interpretation of the Latin American story. His *Open Veins of Latin America* is a classic work (English trans: Monthly Review Press, 1973) while his more recent trilogy *Memory of Fire* (original edition: Siglo Veintiuno, Mexico City, 1982, 1984, 1986) offers a unique tapestry of Latin American history since before the conquest. Other useful political and sociological overviews of Latin America with particular emphasis on dependency are *Politics and Dependency in the Third World: The Case of Latin America* by Ronaldo Munck (Zed Books, 1984), *Theories of Underdevelopment* by Ian Roxborough (Macmillan, 1979) and *Latin American Society* by Tessa Cubitt (Longman, 1988). A more personal introduction by the most experienced journalist writing on Latin America in these islands is *Latin Americans* by Hugh O'Shaughnessy (BBC, 1988).

On Central America, a comprehensive introduction is provided by *Power in the Isthmus* by James Dunkerley (Verso, 1988). Another more accessible narrative with particular focus on US intervention is *Under the Eagle* by Jenny Pearce (Latin America Bureau, updated edition 1982).

On particular countries and themes, the publications of the Latin America Bureau (LAB) provide compact introductions. Of particular usefulness for this book were *Columbus: His Enterprise* by Hans Koning (LAB edition 1991), *Chile: The Pinochet Decade* (1983), *Peru: Paths to Poverty* (1985), *Brazil: State and Struggle* (1982), *Bolivia: Coup d'État* (1980) and *Falklands/Malvinas: Whose Crisis?* (1982).

The more critical Latin American viewpoint on 1492 is provided by the stimulating series of essays *1492-1992: The Voice of the Victims* edited by Leonardo Boff and Virgil Elizondo, which is the December 1990 issue of the international theological journal *Concilium* (SCM Press, 1990). Other works worth consulting on the pre-Columbian cultures are *The Ancient Sun Kingdoms of the Americas* by Victor Wolfgang von Hagen (Paladin, 1973), *The First Americans* by G.H.S. Bushnell (Thames and Hudson, 1968) and *The History of the Incas* by Alfred Métraux (Random House, 1969).

Some Irish publications on the region include the contributions to the annual Jean Donovan lecture series in UCC: *Guatemala: The Struggle for Democracy* by Piero Gleijeses (Modern History Department, UCC, 1986) and *Witness to the Truth: Church and Dictatorship in Latin America* edited by Dermot Keogh (Hibernian University Press, 1989). *Beyond the Cold War* edited by Dermot Keogh (Hibernian University Press, 1990) also contains some important essays on Latin America. *Romero: El Salvador's Martyr* by Dermot Keogh (Dominican Publications, 1981) contains useful background on the 1932 peasant revolt in El Salvador and *Lessons in Liberation* by Peadar Kirby (Dominican Publications, 1981) is an introduction to the new model of church in Latin America. *Church for Liberation: A Pastoral Portrait of the Church in Brazil* by David Regan (Dominican Publications, 1987) is a revealing insight into how one church was changed. *What is Liberation Theology?* is an introduction by a leading Irish theologian, Fr Denis Carroll (Mercier Press, 1987). Two Irish experiences of Nicaragua are provided by *Light after Darkness: An Experience of Nicaragua* by Betty Purcell (Attic Press, 1989) and *Dialann ó Nicearagua* by Peadar Kirby (An Clóchomhar, 1990).

Very useful up-to-date sources are the publications of Nacla and Latinamerica Press. Nacla publishes bi-monthly in-depth studies of countries and of themes which uncover in a thoroughly researched way the real forces shaping Latin America. Not surprisingly, the magazine was under constant pressure from the US authorities during the Reagan administration (Nacla: Report on the Americas, 151 West 19th Street, 9th Floor, New York, NY 10011, USA). Latinamerica Press, published in Lima, Peru,

is a weekly update on general developments in the region with particular emphasis on grassroots struggles. Its special issues on themes such as the military, women, youth, indigenous, the environment and the debt crisis, published roughly every quarter, are especially valuable as sources (Latinamerica Press, Apartado 5594, Lima 100, Peru).

Part Two:
Ireland and Latin America

Sources for the Irish in Latin America are very fragmentary and limited to particular aspects. *Ireland and America: Their Early Associations, 1500-1640* by David B. Quinn (Liverpool University Press, 1991) provides some information on Latin America and the Caribbean. The 1930 volume of *The Irish Jesuit Yearbook* contains a section by Fr John MacErlean SJ on Irish Jesuits who served in Latin America in the 17th and 18th centuries. *The Lost Paradise* by Philip Caraman (Sidgwick & Jackson, 1975) on the Jesuit Reductions in Paraguay gives more information on the role of Fr Thomas Field.

Fr Aubrey Gwynn SJ did a lot to expand our knowledge about Irish involvement in the West Indies and his "First Irish Priests in the New World" (*Studies* 1932, pp 213-228) and "Early Irish emigration to the West Indies (1612-43)" (*Studies* 1929, pp 377-393, 648-663) are of particular interest. On Cromwellian deportation see Gwynn (*Studies* 1930, pp 607-623) and D. Murphy SJ (*Irish Ecclesiastical Record*, 1893, pp 609-613, 744-750). On the Black Irish of Jamaica see Gwynn (*Studies* 1932, p. 694). On Irish settlements on the Amazon see *English and Irish Settlements on the River Amazon 1550 to 1646* edited by Joyce Lorimer (Hakluyt Society and Cambridge University Press, 1989). The document of Bernard O'Brien from which extensive quotes are taken is reproduced in this book (pp 263-8).

The expert on the Irish in Montserrat is Michael D. Higgins TD who made a film for Channel 4 on the subject. He has a paper in *The Emigrant Experience* (Galway Labour History Group, 1991, pp 56-67) together with a reply by Fred Johnston (pp 68, 69). The interview with the Montserrat poet, E.A. Markham, was in *The Irish Times* of 4 April 1991. The correspondence of the Irish Dominicans on St Croix was edited by Fr Hugh Fenning OP in *Archivium Hibernicum*, 1963, pp

75-122. On the Irish regiment in Mexico see "An Irish Regiment in Mexico 1768-1771" by W.S. Murphy (*The Irish Sword* 1956, pp 257-263).

Sources consulted for the Irish in Argentina include the special centenary issue of *The Southern Cross* (1975) and "Irish Migration to Argentina" an undergraduate geography thesis by Pat McKenna, kindly lent by the author, which is available in the Geography Library, St Patrick's College, Maynooth. Sources for the Irish in the South American wars of independence include "Irish Soldiers in South America 1818-30" by Eric Lambert (*Studies* 1969, pp 376-395) and "Bolívar and his Irish Legionaires" by W.J. Williams (*Studies* 1929, pp 619-32).

Ireland and the Irish in Maritime History by John de Courcy Ireland (Glendale Press, 1986) contains information on the Irish who played a role in South American maritime history. See also the same author on Thomas Charles Wright (*The Irish Sword* 1964, pp 271-275). For the Irish regiment in Brazil 1826-28, see Frederic von Allendorfer (*The Irish Sword* 1957, pp 28-31). For St Patrick's battalion see "San Patricio Deserters in the Mexican War 1847" by Richard Blaine McCornack (*The Irish Sword* 1958, pp 246-55). For James J. O'Kelly, see *La Tierra del Mambí*, introduction by Fernando Ortíz (Centenario 1868, Instituto del Libro, Havana, 1968).

Much of the material for Chapters 9 to 11 is based on interviews with those quoted since written sources, apart from newspaper articles, are very sparse. Even where written sources are available, for example on the Irish missionary movement, they tend to neglect the involvement in Latin America. See in particular *The Irish Missionary Movement: A Historical Survey, 1830-1980* by Edmund M. Hogan (Gill & Macmillan, 1990). On the Cork mission to Peru, see *Mission to the New World* by Fr Thomas Kelleher (Icon Communications, Cork). This contains the text of Pope John XXIII's letter to the Irish bishops. A good history of the missionary movement in Latin America but with an almost exclusive focus on US involvement is *Mission to Latin America: The Successes and Failures of a Twentieth Century Crusade* by Gerald M. Costello (Orbis Books, 1979).

Index

import substitution industrialis-
ation 10, 42-3, 48, 55
Incas 23-4, 74, 140
inquilino 94
Inquisition 26, 80
Inter-American Development Bank
60
International Court of Justice 159
International Fund for Ireland 175
International Monetary Fund 60,
62, 69
Ireland-Chile Support Committee
155, 178
Ireland-Cuba Friendship Society
157
Ireland-US Chamber of Commerce
163, 175-7
Irish Army 122
Irish Brazil Solidarity Group 157,
178
Irish Congress of Trade Unions
152, 153
Irish El Salvador Support
Committee 149, 156, 178
Irish European Chamber of
Commerce 129
Irish missionaries 133, 136-42
Irish Network on Debt and
Development 169
Irish Nicaragua Support Group
149, 156-7, 178
Irish policy on Latin America 120-
6
Irish Theological Association 143
Irish Times, The 158
Irish trade with Latin America 127-
30

Jamaica 89-90, 137
Jefferson Smurfit Group 129
Jesuits:
    Centre for Faith and Justice 147
    colleges 82, 83
    Dublin parishes 144
    expulsion 82
    Irish in Latin America 82-3
    Luis Espinal House 144
    Paraguayan province 81
    Republic of Paraguay 27-8
    Rutilio Grande community 144
João IV, 87, 88
John Paul II 21, 59-60
John XXIII, 137, 139

Johnson, L B 54
Jordan, Tom OP 144
justicialismo 47

Keating, Diago Nicolau 103
Keen, Benjamin 36
Kennedy, Hyacinth OP 91
Kennedy, John F 53, 176
Keogh, Dermot 168
Kerins, Fr Noel 146
Kilbeggan 105
Kilmore Quay 105
Kiltegans 138
Kirkpatrick, Jeane 122
Kirwan, Lawrence 108
Korea 137

Labour Party 160
Lamb, Alfie 134, 135
Land League 109
Lara, Gen Guillermo Rodriguez 58
Latin America Solidarity Com-
mittee 157
Lautaro 102
Lea, Francis SJ 83
legacy of conquest 16-18
Legion of Mary 133-6
Leguia, Augusto B 118
Lemass, Sean 176
Lenihan, Brian 119-20
Leny, William SJ 82
Lewis, Thomas SJ 83
liberation theology 20, 143
Lillis, Michael 121
Little, P J 118
Llosa, Mario Vargas 20, 61, 73
Lomé Convention 130-1, 153
López, Carlos Antonio 35-6
López, Francisco Solano 36, 112
Los Angeles Times 163, 176
Loughrea 107
L'Ouverture, Toussaint 32
Lynch, Elisa A 112-3
Lynch, Jack 176
Lynch, Michael SJ 83
Lynch, Noel 35
Lynch, Patricio 102-3
Lynch, Thomas SJ 82
Lynch, William SJ 83

MacDonagh, Oliver 95
Mac Giolla Riabhaigh, Cornelius SJ
82